THE WAY
IT WAS
in NEW ENGLAND

THE WAY IT WAS

in NEW ENGLAND

Clarence P. Hornung

White Light, Isles of Shoals

SMITHMARK

This edition published in 1992 by SMITHMARK Publishers, Inc.
16 East 32nd Street, New York NY 10016

Printed by special arrangement with
William S. Konecky Associates, Inc.

SMITHMARK books are available for bulk purchase for
sales promotion and premium use. For details write
or telephone the Manager of Special Sales, SMITHMARK
Publishers, Inc., 16 East 32nd Street, New York NY 10016.
(212) 532-6600.

ISBN 0-8317-9357-0

Printed in the United States of America

CONTENTS

NEW ENGLAND

1. ALONG MAINES ROCK-BOUND SHORES   1

2. BOSTON . . . CRADLE OF LIBERTY
   . . . ATHENS OF AMERICA   15

3. A CLUSTER OF TOWNS SURROUNDS
   THE HUB   37

4. HIGH PEAKS & HIGHLIGHTS
   IN SCENIC NEW HAMPSHIRE   57

5. AMID VERMONT'S GREEN HILLS   67

6. RHODE ISLAND'S BUSY TOWNS
   & SEAPORTS   77

7. THE CONNECTICUT VALLEY
   & VILLAGES   86

List of Authors   103

Along Maine's Rock-bound Coast

MOUNT DESERT ISLAND . . . "THE OVENS" . . .

GREAT HEAD . . . EAGLE LAKE . . . SOMES'

POND . . . CADILLAC MOUNTAIN . . . PORTLAND

. . . CASCO BAY . . . AUGUSTA . . . OLDTOWN . . .

PENOBSCOT, KENNEBEC AND ANDROSCOGGIN

RIVERS . . . CAMDEN AND VICINITY . . .

PORTSMOUTH AND THE ISLES OF SHOALS,

NEW HAMPSHIRE

CASTLE HEAD, MOUNT DESERT

Along Maine's Rock-bound Coast

WITH A JIGSAWED COASTLINE of 2,500 miles, and countless offshore islands, Maine is the most spectacular—as well as the largest—of the New England states. Bounded on the east by Canada's provinces of Quebec and New Brunswick, with the St. John and the St. Croix rivers forming part of the international boundary, Maine shares its state-side boundary only with New Hampshire. To the east lies the Bay of Fundy; to the south, the vast Atlantic.

Ancient ages laid down a bedrock of sandstone, shale, and limestone, crystallized by molten granite. While the softer rock generally eroded into valleys, the most resilient formed Maine's mountainous west, and, on the east, the mountains of Mount Desert. Long drift ridges, deposited by the receding glaciers, dammed the valleys and created Maine's amazing endowment of more than 2,200 lakes, etching out rugged waterways.

In Frenchman's Bay, just off the coast of Maine southeast of Bangor, Mount Desert Island stands in breath-taking majesty, surrounded by seas, crowned with mountains—the only area along the Atlantic coast where mountains stand close to the sea. Ever since the end of the 1880s, Mount Desert has been one of New England's most famous tourist resorts as well as a leading fishing and lumbering area. Acacia National park occupies the greater part of the island. Among numerous harbors, those best known are Southwest and Northeast, with—on the eastern shore—Bar Harbor, so named for the sandy bar which connects it with the northernmost island in the Porcupine group.

The village, East Eden, is the tourist center. Most visitors booked for a holiday at East Eden set themselves to explore the rocks along the shore, then ascend the Green Mountain for its "thunder-smitten" view. After these tributes to island scenery, hunting and fishing compete with the allure of coastal bays and inlets for the yachtsman's delight—"A yachting party might spend an entire summer in threading the mazes of hundred-harbored Maine," as Whittier described it.

Points of exceptional interest are the "ovens," about seven miles up the bay, and "Schooner Head," "Great Head," and "Otter Creek Cliffs" on the seaward shore. While some of the Ovens are only slight indentations, others are large enough to hold thirty to forty people. At low tide, the shore at the "Ovens" is a favorite picnic ground for summer visitors. They lunch in the caves, saunter through the forests on the cliffs, gather harebells and roses, and search the rocky shore for weird sea creatures brought in by the waves.

It was Champlain, landing here in 1604, who named the island. In 1613 a French Jesuit mission and colony were established, but in the same year the British destroyed the settlement, claiming the land because of earlier explorations made by Cabot.

Human occupation of the peninsula, now known as Maine, goes back to prehistoric times, as burial mounds of the Red Paint people—found in the south-central part of the state—indicate. Afterward, the Indians came and left tremendous heaps of shells, said to date back 1,000 to 5,000 years. When the white explorers arrived, there were friendly Abnaki Indians settled on certain coastal and inland sections. Norsemen may have known Maine's coast long before the arrival of British, French, and Spanish mariners, who preceded Champlain's settlement at the mouth of the St. Croix.

From the extreme southwestern tip of the state to its northeastern boundary, the land is threaded with rivers—the Kennebec, Penobscott, Androscoggin, Saco, and the St. Croix being the most important. They trace their intricate courses over the land and pour into the Atlantic. The St. John, after meandering through northern Maine, flows into New Brunswick.

Maine's generally poor soil and short growing season operate against a prosperous agriculture, and the lack of coal and steel is a handicap to extensive manufacturing. But the matchless majesty of Maine's seacoasts and mountains, and its fish and wild game, hold an irresistible lure for visitors, creating a lucrative tourist industry. The protected harbors, which serve as fishing ports, the rapid rivers providing power for factories, and the still-extensive lumber resources are factors important to Maine's economy.

From the days when her straight white pines provided masts for the British navy, lumbering has dominated Maine's industry and export trade. Although the virgin timber now is largely cut, and forest fires have taken a devastating toll, conservation and reforestation enable Maine to still manufacture pulpwood and paper. Maine gained her name of the "Pine Tree State" from the once-great stands of white pine which are now almost extinct. Forests of spruce, fir, hemlock, and hardwoods are still to be found in most parts of the state. Especially in the lesser populated northern counties that are sheltered by lakes and woods, moose, deer, black bears, and smaller game abound. Fowl and fish are plentiful, and Maine lobsters are famous across the nation. There is heavy concentration on market gardening, poultry raising, and dairying to meet the needs of local and New England markets. The cultivation of potatoes, especially in Aroostook County, has spread Maine's fame far beyond New England. A highly profitable timber trade is carried on with Europe and Asia.

More than two thousand miles of twisted and indented coastline form the sea-swept shores of the Pine Tree State . . .

As the coast-dweller looks from his cottage window, or the tourist gazes from the piazza of his hotel over some portion of the restless beauty and indescribable blending of things that is presented along the Maine shore, he is thinking almost wholly of the present and very little of the past. He sees numerous headlands and islands in a setting of watery coves and thoroughfares that wind in and between and out, all connecting somehow with the open sea. The profusion of scenery possesses his mind. The view extends far away and there are islands always. Some have high walls and bold projecting bluffs; others recede gently and are so low that they scarcely seem to rise above the water's brim; nearly all are dark and distinct in their covering of dense evergreen. A blue mountain range is seen in the eastern far-away. At the moment the atmosphere is peaceful and restful. The water-ripples lap and sparkle. The distant steamboat, followed by a trail of smoke, plows its course swiftly and gracefully, and all the little snatches of detached landscape are mantled in their pleasantest hues.

No, our fisherman or tourist thinks not of the past. He is engrossed completely in the scene before him. Perhaps he has forgotten the legends and history that make Maine one of the most interesting of all our commonwealths; or, perchance, in the busy rush of life's routine he has given little heed to legends and history.

In times comparatively remote, it is said that the adventurous Northmen visited our continent and many of us believe that their dark ships sailed the waters of the Gulf of Maine.

L. WHITNEY ELKINS
The Story of Maine
1924

THE CLIFFS NEAR "THE OVENS"

. . . dotted with hundreds of isles and inlets as the swift-flowing Penobscot, Kennebec, and Androscoggin rush to greet the sea

THE "SPOUTING HORN" IN A STORM

They say here that great waves reach this coast in threes. Three great waves, then an indeterminate run of lesser rhythms, then three great waves again. On Celtic coasts it is the seventh wave that is seen coming like a king out of the grey, cold sea. The Cape tradition, however, is no half-real, half-mystical fancy, but the truth itself. Great waves do indeed approach this beach by threes. Again and again have I watched three giants roll in one after the other out of the Atlantic, cross the outer bar, break, form again, and follow each other in to fulfillment and destruction on this solitary beach. Coast Guard crews are all well aware of this triple rhythm and take advantage of the lull that follows the last wave to launch their boats. It is true that there are single giants as well. I have been roused by them in the night. Waked by their tremendous and unexpected crash, I have sometimes heard the last of the heavy overspill, sometimes only the loud, withdrawing roar. After the roar came a briefest pause, and after the pause the return of ocean to the night's long cadences. Such solitary titans, flinging their green tons down upon a quiet world, shake beach and dune. Late one September night, as I sat reading, the very father of all waves must have flung himself down before the house, for the quiet of the night was suddenly overturned by a gigantic, tumbling crash and an earthquake rumbling; the beach trembled beneath the avalanche, the dune shook, and my house so shook on its dune that the flame of a lamp quivered and pictures jarred on the wall.

HENRY BESTON

The Outermost House

*Majestic Cadillac crowns Mount Desert Island,
highest peak on the long Atlantic seaboard from
downeast Maine to the Florida Keys . . .*

I never knew, or had forgotten how much of Maine sticks up like a thumb into Canada...We know so little of our own geography. Why, Maine extends northward almost to the mouth of the St. Lawrence, and its upper border is perhaps a hundred miles north of Quebec...As I drove north through the little towns and the increasing forest rolling away to the horizon, the season changed quickly and out of all proportion. Perhaps it was my getting away from the steadying hand of the sea, and also perhaps I was getting very far north. The houses had a snow-beaten look, and many were crushed and deserted, driven to earth by the winters. Except in the towns there was evidence of a population which had once lived here and farmed and had its being and had been driven out. The forests were marching back, and where farm wagons once had been only the big logging trucks rumbled along. And the game had come back, too; deer strayed on the roads and there were marks of bear.

JOHN STEINBECK

*Travels with Charley
in Search of America*

GREAT HEAD

EAGLE LAKE

. . . where forest-clad headlands and granite cliffs, side by side, unite to create vistas of unparalleled beauty and unforgettable drama

THUNDER CAVE

Mount Desert has a unique combination of mountain and sea that sets it apart from all other resorts. Unique, too, is Bar Harbor's strange combination of mountainous social elegances and shaggy simplicity, which leads summer visitors to build magnificent mansions in which to entertain admiring friends; then to build log cabins far off in the deep woods to which they sulkily retire to escape the social activities made necessary by their mansions. From Champlain, who first gave the island its name, down to John Greenleaf Whittier, men have spoken as highly of the beauties of Mount Desert as it's possible to speak. "From the summit of Green Mountain," wrote an anonymous visitor in 1866, "the view is one of unparalleled wonder. Half ocean, half land, and the middle distance a bright mosaic of island and bay, it stretches from far Katahdin at the north, a hundred and twenty miles as the crow flies, to an unlimited distance over the sea."

KENNETH ROBERTS
Trending Into Maine, 1938

VIEW FROM VIA MALA, AT "THE OVENS"

EAGLE CLIFF, SOMES' SOUND

Beyond Cape Elizabeth and Portland Head Light, the blue waters of Casco Bay beckon, studded with islands—one for every day in the year . . .

In the long, covered walk that bridged the gorge between the lighthouse and the house, we played in stormy days; and every evening it was a fresh excitement to watch the lighting of the lamps, and think how far the lighthouse sent its rays, and how many hearts it gladdened with assurance of safety. As I grew older I was allowed to kindle the lamps sometimes myself. That was indeed a pleasure. So little a creature as I might do that much for the great world! But by the fireside our best pleasure lay,— with plants and singing birds and books and playthings and loving care and kindness the cold and stormy season wore itself at last away, and died into the summer calm. We hardly saw a human face beside our own all winter; but with the spring came manifold life to our lonely dwelling,—human life among other forms. Our neighbors from Star rowed across; the pilot-boat from Portsmouth steered over, and brought us letters, newspapers, magazines, and told us the news of months. The faint echoes from the far-off world hardly touched us little ones. We listened to the talk of our elders, "Winfield Scott and Santa Anna!" "The war in Mexico!" "The famine in Ireland!" It all meant nothing to us. We heard the reading aloud of details of the famine, and saw tears in the eyes of the reader, and were vaguely sorry; but the fate of Red Riding-Hood was much more near and dreadful to us.

WHITE HEAD.

PORTLAND HARBOR AND ISLANDS

EVERGREEN LANDING, WHITE HEAD, PORTLAND HEAD LIGHT

*. . . while just across Maine's southernmost
Kittery Point, Portsmouth remembers her past,
John Paul Jones, and its glorious naval victories*

APPLEDORE ISLAND.

STAR ISLAND.

PORTSMOUTH, NH

PORTSMOUTH AND ISLES OF SHOALS

APPLEDORE ISLAND, WHALE ROCK LIGHT, CHURCH STAR ISLAND

Often, in pleasant days, the head of the family sailed away to visit the other islands, sometimes taking the children with him, oftener going alone, frequently not returning till after dark. The landing at White Island is so dangerous that the greatest care is requisite, if there is any sea running, to get ashore in safety. Two long and very solid timbers about three feet apart are laid from the boat-house to low-water mark, and between those timbers the boat's bow must be accurately steered; if she goes to the right or the left, woe to her crew unless the sea is calm! Safely lodged in the slip, as it is called, she is drawn up into the boat house by a capstan, and fastened securely. The lighthouse gave no ray to the dark rock below it; sending its beams far out to sea, it left us at its foot in greater darkness for its lofty light. How sweet the summer wind blew, how softly splashed the water round me, how refreshing was the odor of the sparkling brine!

CELIA THAXTER

Phoenixlike, Portland has risen many times from Indian raids, British bombardment, and catastrophic fires to become Maine's largest city

Any description of Portland is likely to begin with its scenic charm. It is little wonder that the new comer is pleased with its insular beauty, its abrupt headlands, and the sinuous windings of its shores. A true explorer hereabouts finds no monotony, no dearth of variety. As he overlooks the eastern slopes of Munjoy Hill the impressions that come crowding into his mind can not be easily forgotten. He is in one of the most exquisite little corners of Portland's park system. From his vantage point the land terrace descends sharply to the sea-water many feet below. Some cannon, shrubbery, and a curving driveway on the brow of the hill mark the site of old Fort Allen, one of the principal defenses of the city in the War of 1812. The broad, flawless street to the north overlooking the bay is the Eastern Promenade. But the tourist is thinking chiefly of the grand prospect before him. It is one of the moments when he realizes the narrow limitations of his own mind, an occasion of enjoyment mingled with the longing for perceptive powers great enough to comprehend and appreciate fully the entire panorama before his eyes instead of feeling that he can grasp it only imperfectly at best.

L. WHITNEY ELKINS
The Story of Maine
1924

CITY OF PORTLAND, FROM THE HARBOR

CITY HALL, MARKET SQUARE, PORTLAND

Native son Longfellow sings Portland's praises, writing in My Lost Youth: *"Often I think of the beautiful town that is seated by the sea . . ."*

VIEW IN CONGRESS STREET, PORTLAND

At the opposite extremity of the old city — the West End — is another terrace hill, bolder even than its eastern fellow, that is called Bramhall's Hill. Just back from the steep descent of the terrace a perfectly finished roadway extends through another beautiful strip of Portland's park system. This street is the Western Promenade. Here also the first impressions coming to the mind are too vivid to be forgotten. The tourist feels that here is a place of remarkable beauty. The walks and smoothly mown grass are pleasing evidences of the city's care. The wealthiest residential section of Portland extends back from the Western Promenade. There is abundant evidence that this locality has assumed more pretentious airs than it was wont to present when George Bramhall operated his tannery here in the earlier history of the town. The old order has passed and made way for the new.

L. WHITNEY ELKINS
The Story of Maine
1924

JUNCTION OF FREE AND CONGRESS STREETS, PORTLAND

*State-of-Mainers point pridefully to their Capitol,
whose building by noted architect
Charles Bulfinch was started back in 1829*

A whole fleet of schooners and packets plied regularly between Augusta and Boston, and a healthy commercial traffic developed. It was not at all unusual to see twenty-five or more ships docked at the Augusta wharves, even though she did seem to be an inland city. This lasted until the arrival of the railroad, which competed so successfully with the shipping that now no boats go to Augusta. However, by this time (1827) Augusta had become the capital of the state; and although she is an industrial city with over forty enterprises, it is as the capital that she is best known today. The Capitol was begun in 1829. It's a noble and beautiful edifice designed by Charles Bulfinch of Boston and constructed of Hallowell granite, which is unusually fine—a clear gray marked with black tourmaline specks and bearing very little mica. The gold figure on top of the dome represents Wisdom, a hopeful choice for any building housing a governing body, I would say. The Capitol contains a Hall of Flags, as well as the very excellent State Library, which performs an unusually good and efficient service in supplying books to people in isolated areas away from the ordinary sources. I used to live in the backwoods myself, and I don't know how I would have got through the long, snowbound winters without the book boxes from the State Library.

LOUISE DICKINSON RICH

The Coast of Maine

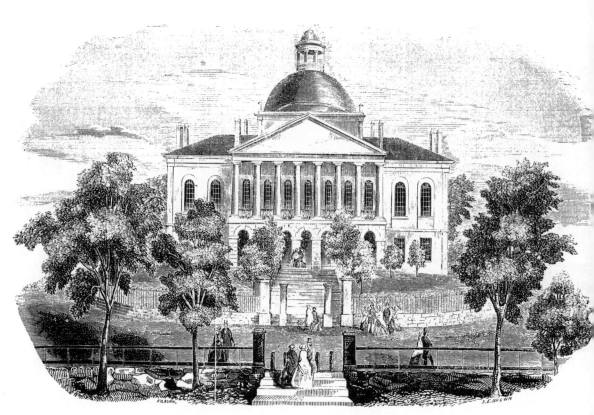

STATE HOUSE AT AUGUSTA, MAINE

UNITED STATES ARSENAL, AUGUSTA

Besides lumbering and logging, the Penobscot's fame derives from its ancient Indian tribes, whose annual powwow and palaver are a cherished tradition

OLDTOWN, ON THE PENOBSCOT RIVER, MAINE

Within a dozen miles of Bangor we passed through the villages of Stillwater and Oldtown, built at the falls of the Penobscot, which furnish the principal power by which the Maine woods are converted into lumber. The mills are built directly over and across the river. Here is a close jam, a hard rub at all seasons; and then the once green tree, long since white, I need not say as the driven snow, but as a driven log, becomes lumber merely. Here your inch, your two- and your three-inch stuff begin to be, and Mr. Sawyer marks off those spaces which decide the destiny of so many prostrate forests. Through this steel riddle, more or less coarse, is the arrowy Maine forest, from Ktaadn and Chesuncook, and the headwaters of the St. John, relentlessly sifted, till it comes out boards, clapboards, laths and shingles such as the wind can take, still perchance to be slit and slit again till men get a size that will suit. There were in 1837, as I read, two hundred and fifty sawmills on the Penobscot and its tributaries above Bangor, the greater part of them in this immediate neighborhood, and they sawed two hundred millions of feet of boards annually. To this is to be added the lumber of the Kennebec, Androscoggin, Saco, Passamaquoddy and other streams.

HENRY DAVID THOREAU
The Maine Woods, 1864

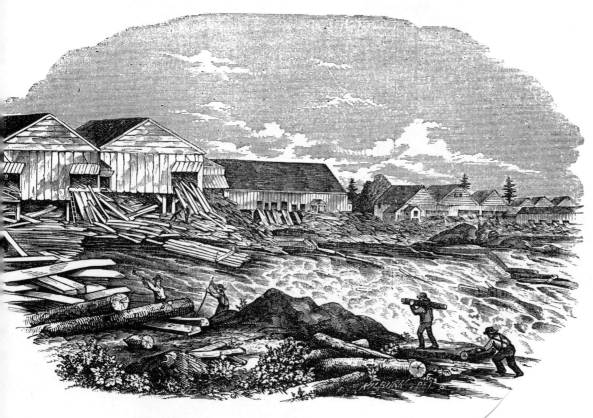

SAW-MILLS ON THE PENOBSCOT RIVER, OLDTOWN

About halfway up the Maine coast lies Camden, near Rockland and Rockport—names descriptive of the rugged terrain—overlooking Penobscot Bay and its many islands: Vinalhaven, its largest

It is customary to speak of Maine as a rugged state. The adjective is deserved, as this witness can testify. I have met her rugged yeomanry and I have skirted her rugged shore line; have viewed her rugged mountains and ranged her rugged forests...A few years of Maine politics would make almost anyone indifferent to the rigors of the climate and the hardships of the wilderness.

IRVIN S. COBB

We were standing where there was a fine view of the harbor and its long stretches of shore all covered by the great army of the pointed firs, darkly cloaked and standing as if they waited to embark. As we looked far seaward among the outer islands, the trees seemed to march seaward still, going steadily over the heights and down to the water's edge.

SARAH ORNE JEWETT

CAMDEN AND VICINITY

Boston ...
Cradle of Liberty ...
Athens of America

THE COMMON . . . FANEUIL HALL . . .

STATE HOUSE . . . CUSTOM HOUSE . . .

BOSTON HARBOR . . . CHELSEA . . .

EAST BOSTON . . . QUINCY MARKET . . .

BACK BAY . . . BLACKSTONE SQUARE . . .

LOUISBURG SQUARE . . . TREMONT STREET . . .

AMAICA POND . . . BOSTON NECK . . .

LOWELL RAILROAD DEPOT . . .

BOSTON AND CAMBRIDGE RAILROAD . . .

CAMBRIDGE . . . HARVARD UNIVERSITY

Boston...
Cradle of Liberty...
Athens of America

BREWER FOUNTAIN, BOSTON COMMON

IT WAS A "BOLD, BALD, BLEAK, TRIPLE-hilled peninsula" to which the Elder, John Winthrop, came in 1630, seeking a site for the main colony of the Massachusetts Bay Company.

One effusive Pilgrim, wandering about in the neighborhood where Charlestown and Bunker Hill now are, declared that the land possessed "rare endowments, dainty hillocks, plains delicate and fair, streams jetting jocundly," but another report described the promontory as "bleak and drear, a hideous wilderness, possessed by barbarous Indians, very cold, sickly, rocky, barren, unfit for culture, likely to make the people miserable."

The newcomers called the area "Tri-Mountain"; the Indians—more poetic—named it "Shawmut," or "Sweet Waters." The earliest settlers, coming from the old Boston of the fens in British Lincolnshire, named the new colony "Boston." Settlers in Charlestown—"suffering from exceeding want of water"—found allure in the Indians' name of

"Sweet Waters" and moved to Boston. They bought land from the owner Reverend, Blackstone, for thirty pounds and, as *Picturesque America* told its readers in 1872, "Boston began to exist with its teeming memories, its dramatic history, steady growth, and its picturesque and romantic aspects."

Certainly few American cities can boast such a rich background, such devotion to learning, such pride in natural endowments, such lusty commercial and industrial development.

Boston's notable ministers and statesmen—the vanguard in American Puritanism as, later, their successors were the ardent champions of Abolition—contributed immeasurably to Boston's intellectual life, until the town became known as the "Athens of America."

The Congregational organization of churches allowed almost every man a say in religious affairs, just as he had in the town meeting in local government. Following the Massachusetts Bay Charter, the legislature and the magistrates gave the colonists a representative system, embodying the seeds of democracy and nationalism.

The city's proud "firsts" are the *Boston Public Latin School,* established in 1630; *Harvard University,* founded in nearby Cambridge in 1636; a *Free Public Library* in 1653; and the first newspaper in the Thirteen Colonies, the *News-Letter,* in 1704. The Boston Public Latin School—attended by many famous men—produced five signers of the Declaration of Independence and four Presidents of Harvard.

Every United States history book is starred with outstanding events from Boston's early days: Boston Massacre, Boston Tea Party, Battle of Bunker Hill; and names like Faneuil Hall, Old North Church, the Old South Meeting House, are equally etched in the nation's memory. Boston's revolutionary heroes—John and Samuel Adams, Paul Revere, Benjamin Franklin, John Hancock, Josiah Quincy, Artemas Ward, and others, are interwoven with the nation's history.

Wooden ships built in Boston carried its name around the world; innumerable fisheries flourished, and the manufacture of shoes and textiles prospered. The port's advantageous location gave Boston supremacy over other New England colonial towns. Just as great Boston fortunes were made in textiles and in boots and shoes, the young clipper boat captains in the China trade often made sizeable fortunes after no more than two or three voyages. Their turnover was immediate and enormous.

There is great charm to Boston Common, for more than two centuries a promenade for grown-ups and playground for children. Occupying nearly 50 acres between Beacon and Boylston Streets, with its lawns as velvety and green as those of boasted London parks, its rows of elms on the Great Mall dating back 150 years, the Common reveals both venerable age and the care with which it is maintained by modern Boston.

Prominent Boston families—Cabots, Lowells, Lodges, and others—made fortunes from shipping, and from mills and factories built on New England rivers. They built substantial homes on Beacon Hill and in the Back Bay sections, and patronized the arts and letters. Despite the conservative tone of their culture, they backed reformers, notably the Abolitionists. Their influence persisted long after the growth of industry brought many immigrants—chiefly Irish at first—and Boston changed from a farm-surrounded commercial city to an industrial metropolis. Where other European settlers in America—from Canada to the Caribbean— thought of themselves as French, English, Dutch, or Spanish, with an expectation of eventually returning "home," the New England settler regarded America as home, convinced that his service to God and English-speaking people was vitally important, and bringing liberty, democracy, and universal education. Cotton Mather, in 1684, is reputed to be the first to apply the name "American" not only to the Indian, but to the colonists.

The water view shows Boston's industrial and commercial character: large, many-windowed factories...tall, smoke-stained chimneys...above the thickly-settled streets from City Point, to South Boston and Chelsea. As in most cities—dating back several centuries—beautiful, modern avenues run into the narrow, crooked streets of colonial days. *Picturesque America* informed its readers: "The almost-mathematically cone-shaped city is actually the most uneven and jagged; its general plan is no plan at all. Many of its thorofares run so crazily that he who travels by them comes almost to his starting point, while others run into 'No thorofare'."

In words somewhat less than transcendental Ralph Waldo Emerson is credited with the comment: "We say the cows have laid out Boston. Well, there are worse surveyors."

18

*In the heart of Boston, noted for its Beacon Hill,
Back Bay, Louisburg Square and many other
residential sections of the city . . .*

Yet the old charm lingers on. You will find it in the lovely old red brick homes of Beacon Hill, with cobblestoned Acorn Street and Louisburg Square, where a little green park is ringed by stately 19th-century houses and gas lampposts. Historic Boston can be seen in an hour or two along the mile-and-a-half Freedom Trail in this most walkable of all American cities: the State House with its 23-carat gold dome, begun from designs by Charles Bulfinch in 1795; the pleasant expanse of the Boston Common, which the town bought as a "trayning field" for the militia and for the "feeding of Cattell" back in the 17th century, and where pirates, witches, and Quakers were hanged from an elm near the Frog Pond; Park Street Church, where William Lloyd Garrison delivered his first antislavery speech in 1829; the Old Granary Burying Ground with the graves of John Hancock, Samuel Adams, and Paul Revere; the Boston Athenaeum, the literary *sanctum sanctorum* of old Boston; King's Chapel, which was the Episcopal place of worship of early British governors and later the first Unitarian church in America; the Old State House and scene of the Boston Massacre; the Old South Meeting House where Bostonians met to protest the British tea tax before staging their famous Tea Party; Faneuil Hall, where Sam Adams and James Otis delivered the fiery speeches that led to Revolution; the Paul Revere House, Boston's oldest wooden frame building (1677); and the Old North Church, immortalized by Longfellow's poem about Revere's midnight ride.

PANORAMIC VIEW

NEAL R. PEIRCE

*The New England States,
1976*

. . . steep, staggered side streets criss-cross with dead-end lanes where unpredictable, classic mansions are often flanked by drab, depressing lodging houses

CITY OF BOSTON

There is nothing in New England corresponding at all to the feudal aristocracies of the Old World. Whether it be owing to the stock from which we were derived, or to the practical working of our institutions, or to the abrogation of the technical "law of honor," which draws a sharp line between the personally responsible class of "gentlemen" and the unnamed multitude of those who are not expected to risk their lives for an abstraction,—whatever be the cause, we have no such aristocracy here as that which grew up out of the military systems of the Middle Ages. What we mean by "aristocracy" is merely the richer part of the community, that live in the tallest houses, drive real carriages, (not "kerridges,") kid-glove their hands, and French-bonnet their ladies' heads, give parties where the persons who call them by the above title are not invited, and have a provokingly easy way of dressing, walking, talking, and nodding to people, as if they felt entirely at home, and would not be embarrassed in the least, if they met the Governor, or even the President of the United States, face to face. Some of these great folks are really well-bred, some of them are only purse-proud and assuming,—but they form a class, and are named as above in the common speech.

OLIVER WENDELL HOLMES
The Autocrat of the Breakfast-Table, 1858

Architecturally, Boston was a living museum of America's changing styles expressed in public buildings from the days of native-born Charles Bulfinch and his influence . . .

The Boston Custom House—the work of Ammi Young—was the first-magnitude star in the galaxy of Boston's Greek Revival buildings. The monolithic columns weigh forty-two tons each. It stood, in 1849, facing the waterfront, but its original charm is entirely lost today under the great tower rising above it. A few of its inner columns now form a kind of modern Stonehenge out in Franklin Park. The old Tremont House, with a Greek facade of white Quincy granite, was the first of many impressive American hotels which appeared during the Greek Revival. It is one of the vanished buildings of Boston which I would like most to have seen. It must have been a noble affair with that great dining room seating two hundred diners at once, its whale-oil lamps, and bathing rooms in the basement. Dickens said of it that "it had more galleries, colonnades, piazzas, and passages than he could remember or the reader believe." It was built by Isaiah Rogers in 1829 and was torn down in true American fashion in the mid-1890's. It was Rogers who designed the Howard Athenaeum, a granite Gothic building off Scollay Square which burned in 1846 and was rebuilt by the same man. A theater where Joseph Jefferson once played, it is known today the world over as the Old Howard. Another example of Rogers's Gothic style is the Unitarian Church in Harvard Square. Such are the beginning of the architectural history of our city.

DAVID MC CORD
About Boston, 1948

THE STATE HOUSE, BOSTON

BOSTON ATHENAEUM

. . . on through the period of Greek Revival when, as Kilhan so charmingly noted, "Boston shed its provincial attitude and began to assume the airs of a metropolis"

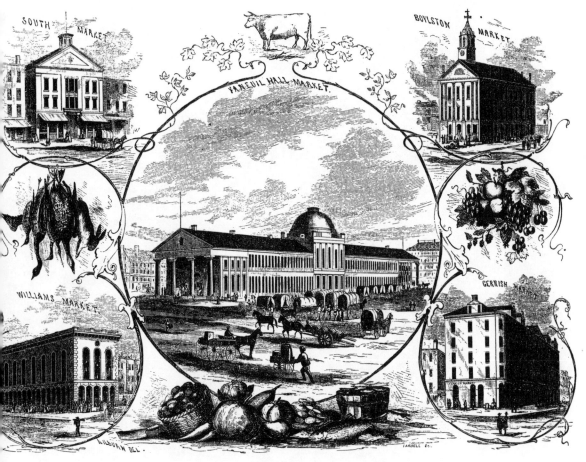

PUBLIC MARKET HOUSES IN BOSTON

"No matter what the period, the style was fixed then, as now, purely and simply by fashion and nothing else. No distinctively American style was ever really in evidence, and quite possibly none ever will be, for as long as people lack definite religious and political convictions, and particularly as long as a lagging philosophy fails to catch up with runaway science, just so long will Americans be unable to create a style of their own as distinctive as the Grecian or the Gothic." This opinion I take verbatim from a remarkable little book of one hundred pages called *Boston after Bulfinch*, by Walter H. Kilham—a book which every Bostonian who cares about his city should find time to read. Mr. Kilham laments the fact that an architect's name is not likely to live long after his death. This is a sad truth indeed. Christopher Wren is the one architect of London that the world at large remembers; Bulfinch is *the* architect of Boston, at least so far as the general public goes. Even one with so assertive a name as Ammi Young is forgotten, though his Greek Revival Custom House has since soared to a height unchallenged till this present moment of renewed and noisy building activity.

DAVID MC CORD

About Boston, 1948

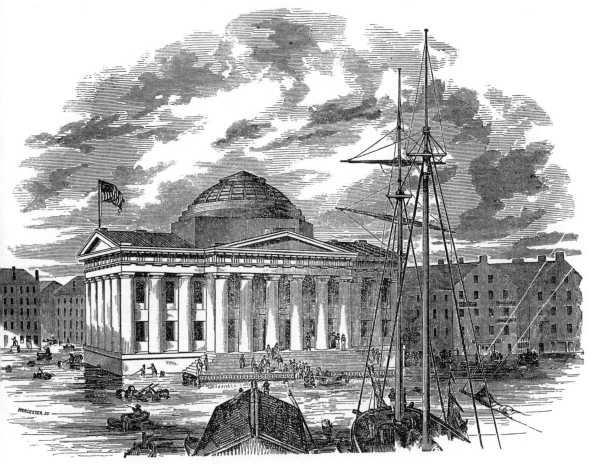

BOSTON CUSTOM HOUSE

Rivers, bridges, docks and wharves mark the maritime complex that is Boston, interlaced with peninsulas and an endless, labyrinthian shoreline . . .

The familiar phrase of one if by land and two if by sea gives numerical emphasis to the Atlantic Ocean. So through the greater part of three centuries the emphasis of Boston has been on the sea that washes almost to her door. By reason of her long, deep-channeled, and intricate harbor, Boston is a riparian city without really enjoying in the larger sense an actual outlook on the ocean; and because of this fact we sometimes forget that she is a seaport city first of all. New York is so very nearly encircled by ships and tugs and barges and ferries, and San Francisco so plainly indented by the Pacific, that we think of them in the maritime sense first and last. Many of us in Boston today can and do go about our business without so much as a sight of any part of the waterfront for months at a time. We know that the waterfront is there.

DAVID MC CORD

About Boston, 1948

VIEW OF CHELSEA FROM EAST BOSTON

LOOKING TOWARD CHELSEA FROM EAST BOSTON

. . . recalling to residents and visitors alike that the city's growth stems from shipping and distributing its harvest of the seas

SCENE ON SOUTH BOSTON BRIDGE

The first area of permanent settlement in the present City of Boston was in the Dock Square section, which is now part of the North End. By the time when the large stream of Irish immigration began, in the eighteen-forties, this area was already solidly build up, and the social leaders of the city were moving from it to outlying parts. This great wave of immigration changed the North End rapidly into a congested tenement district. By 1850 half of the 23,000 inhabitants were Irish, and the proportion increased steadily until 1880, when this was a predominantly Irish district. Soon afterward, however, the Irish population declined rapidly before a new wave of immigration, which came largely from Italy and Russia. In 1880 there were fewer than a thousand Italians in the district, but fifteen years later, the state census listed 7700 Italians, 6800 Irish, 6200 Jews (all but 400 coming from Russia), 1200 British or British Americans (immigrants from England, Scotland, and Canada), and 800 Portuguese. Throughout the early nineteen-hundreds the Italian immigration continued, while the Irish moved out in increasing numbers, and the Jews, though they retained their clothing stores on Salem and Hanover Streets, also sought other places to live.

WILLIAM FOOTE WHYTE,
New England Quarterly, 1939

LAUNCHING OF THE U.S.S. MERRIMAC, FROM THE CHARLESTOWN NAVY YARD

As the principal port on the Atlantic coast, Boston harbor brought prosperity to the Colonies, until Britain's wartime blockade temporarily bottled up its seaborne commerce

The harbor of Boston is filled with islands, most of which have a history that it would be exceedingly interesting to recount. That of Castle Island, on which Fort Independence now stands, is more prominent in colonial and revolutionary annals than any other, both because it was the first island fortified and because it was so accessible from the town. The guns of the Castle were the excuse given by the owners of the tea-ships for not going to sea again with the cargoes which were afterwards destroyed; and this island was the scene of many a fatal duel in the olden time. Thompson's Island is remarkable for its fantastic shape, which has been likened to that of an unfledged chicken, and also for the numerous and protracted controversies that have taken place to settle the ownership of the island in the early days of the colony.

VIEW IN BOSTON HARBOR—ENGLISH MAIL STEAMER GOING TO SEA

*In the heyday of the clipper ships, wealthy merchants
sent their swift vessels sailing the seven seas
to bring back aromatic spices, tea, coffee and rum*

Spectacle Island, so named
from its form, was formerly
used for quarantine purposes,
but is now given up to the
very offensive business of
converting retired car horses
into a variety of useful
products. Most of the islands
were granted by the General
Court, during the first years
of the settlement of Boston,
to persons who agreed to pay
a yearly rental in shillings or
rum for their use. Ultimately
they became private property
either by compounding for the
yearly rent or by a sort of
pre-emption which was
accomplished without the aid
of any other law than that of
possession.

Genre scenes of neighborhood and ethnic blend added a bit of spicy divertissement to otherwise dull street settings . . .

There is one week of October, indeed, when I never fail to recapture a certain boyhood remembrance of the color of Halloween. It comes at the close of evening—usually near a fruit store or a flower shop—just when the office buildings pour their life stream into the streets and people for the moment seem uniformly gay and animate and kindly, and the lights come on with a special brightness and twinkle. This above all is the time not only to talk about but to walk about Boston. It is never again so tranquil in the early morning, when the sun puts a pale bright film across the rooftops and chimneys over the Basin, softening in deep purple-blue the aristocratic outline of the Hill. It is the one time when the dark of evening flows quietly in, as sadness will sometimes drift in and out of a human face. It is the season of the end of something and the promise of something else that is not winter. I think perhaps above all that it is the season of dignity, when unconsciously we tend to match ourselves against the brilliance of nature; when our city, old and new, seems even better than she is—as though she were suddenly housecleaned and painted, and aired by all the winds that blow across her from the land and the sea.

DAVID MC CORD

About Boston, 1973

CORNER OF WINTER, WASHINGTON AND SUMMER STREETS, BOSTON

BOSTON STREET SHOWMEN AND MUSICIANS

. . . and provided top-notch illustrators, like Winslow Homer, the opportunity to depict the everyday happenings in the busy metropolis

THE FOUNTAIN ON BOSTON COMMON

TREMONT STREET, OPPOSITE BOSTON COMMON, JULY 4, 1857

We were a cosmopolitan gang. There were Italians, Scotch, Irish, Bohemians, Jews and nondescripts. Here we received our first lessons in languages. We could curse, for example, in all these idioms, and babble a bit in tongues. Demark, McGovern, Kovar, Donovan...these were as often my companions as were the Wolfsons, Fritzes, Levis and Golds. We knew nothing of racial prejudice; one touch of Nature— usually a top seat in the gallery of the burlesque houses—made us all kin. Later, our education would be completed by our parents; we would learn to hate one another as befits members of a Christian civilization. But in those days we were still savages. Indeed, we were so hopelessly retrograde that we cherished only the usual prejudices against girls. The ones we knew were for the greater part tomboys. I don't remember— memory, of course, is a trickster—a single shy girl out of my entire childhood. It is possible that I myself was shy, and that the boldness of the lasses was simply a relative deduction. We were, I recall, a distinctly sophisticated group. We were crammed with misinformation, it is true, thereby resembling the sophisticates of our adulthood. But we knew that there were things that we were not supposed to know, and we acted as if we knew them. That is almost a formula. And before we realized it, we really knew them...

ISAAC GOLDBERG

American Mercury, 1929

In key cities along the Atlantic seaboard, but especially in Boston—citadel of periodical publishing, landmark areas were singled out and illustrated in detail

Anyone who presumes to write about Boston runs the risk of being branded a literary poacher. You see, the city has been sequestrated as a kind of game preserve by the author of *H.M. Pulham, Esq.* Anecdotal rights are fiefed out (in a manor of speaking) to Mr. Cleveland Amory, and thus Boston has become a strictly posted property with seignorial dues payable at the end of every royalty period. I have no wish to disturb this highly profitable arrangement between two fellow authors—but look, I saw the place first. May I not be permitted (just this once) to mention Beacon Street, Commonwealth Avenue and Scollay Square without risking a plagiarism suit? I'll take the chance anyway. To paraphrase Van Wyck Brooks' remark about Bronson Alcott: "Who can expel a man from the Garden of Eden that exists behind his own brow?"

MERCANTILE LIBRARY, SUMMER STREET, BOSTON

HENRY MORTON ROBINSON
Massachusetts, in
American Panorama, 1960

CORNER OF COURT AND TREMONT STREETS, WITH NEW IRON BUILDING

*Not restricted to buildings and relics of the past,
pictures of hotels and theatres provided readers
with a stimulating familiarity with the contemporary scene*

ENTRANCE TO THE NEW BOSTON THEATRE, WASHINGTON STREET

BLACKSTONE SQUARE, BOSTON

The city attracted architects (H.H. Richardson), gave birth to painters (Winslow Homer), created music ("the Boston classicists"), and nourished thinkers and writers—William Dean Howells, the Adams clan, John Boyle O'Reilly, who made *The Pilot* into an international paper, Robert Grant the conservative, B.O. Flower the radical, Borden Parker Bowne, Edgar Brightman, Dallas Lore Sharp, and others. Across the Charles was the brilliant Harvard faculty. The *Atlantic Monthly* continued to be prestigious. The tradition of Emerson and Thoreau still flourished—in the Free Religious Association with its two magazines, in Benjamin R. Tucker, philosophical anarchist and writer for the *Globe,* in B.O. Flower's *The Arena Magazine,* humorless but radical, in a performance of an upsetting foreign play, *A Doll's House,* in 1889, and an upsetting native play, *Margaret Fleming* (in Lynn, 1890) by James A. Herne. Young Hamlin Garland, penniless, came out of the West to read strong literature in the Boston Public Library, the director of which admitted that of course he had anarchist books on his shelves that any mature person could borrow. Flower brought out his *Progressive Men, Women and Movements* in 1914, the year the Twentieth Century Club, founded as that century dawned, published a survey of movements from 1884 to 1914. Nor should it be forgotten that Boston during these years nourished the Mugwumps and the Anti-Imperialist League.

The Athens of America,
from *The Many Voices of
Boston, 1975*

At the midway point in the 19th century, publishers were issuing street and mercantile directories, enlarged annually to keep pace with the city's growth

When I got into the streets upon this Sunday morning, the air was so clear, the houses were so bright and gay, the signboards were painted in such gaudy colours, the gilded letters were so very golden, the bricks were so very red, the stone was so very white, the blinds and area railings were so very green, the knobs and plates upon the street doors were so marvellously bright and twinkling, and all so slight and unsubstantial in appearance, that every thoroughfare in the city looked exactly like a scene in a pantomime. It rarely happens in the business streets that a tradesman—if I may venture to call anybody a tradesman where everybody is a merchant—resides above his store; so that many occupations are often carried on in one house, and the whole front is covered with boards and inscriptions. As I walked along, I kept glancing up at these boards, confidently expecting to see a few of them change into something; and I never turned a corner suddenly without looking out for the Clown and Pantaloon, who, I had no doubt, were hiding in a doorway or behind some pillar close at hand.

CHARLES DICKENS
American Notes, 1842

EAST AND WEST SIDES, FROM COURT STREET TO THE COMMON

PANORAMIC VIEW OF TREMONT STREET, BOSTON

Some popular weekly journals went a step further, offering their readers graphic illustrations of important downtown buildings clearly identified

TREMONT TEMPLE. MONTGOMERY PLACE. GLEASON'S PUBLISHING HALL. BROMFIELD STREET.

PAVILION HOTEL REED'S MUSIC STORE.

TREMONT HOUSE. BEACON STREET. ALBION HOTEL.

There are many clubs at Boston. M. Chastellux speaks of a particular club held once a week. I was at it several times, and was much pleased with their politeness to strangers, and the knowledge displayed in their conversation.

One of the principal pleasures of the inhabitants consists in little parties for the country, among families and friends. The principal expence of the parties, especially after dinner, is tea. In this, as in their whole manner of living, the Americans in general resemble the English. Punch, warm and cold, before dinner; excellent beef, and Spanish and Bordeaux wines, cover their tables, always solidly and abundantly served. Spruce beer, excellent cyder, and Philadelphia porter, precede the wines. . . .

JEAN PIERRE BRISSOT DE WARVILLE
Happy Boston, 1788

*Long periods of severe winter weather gave
New Englanders, youngsters and oldsters alike, a
chance to enjoy the thrills of sleighing and skating*

A hard, dull bitterness
    of cold,
That checked, mid-
    vein, the circling race
Of life-blood in the
    sharpened face,
The coming of the
    snow-storm told.
The wind blew east: we
    heard the roar
Of Ocean on his wintry
    shore,
And felt the strong
    pulse throbbing
    there
Beat with low rhythm our
    inland air...
In starry flake, and
    pellicle,
All day the hoary meteor
    fell;
And, when the second
    morning shone,
We looked upon a world
    unknown,
On nothing we could call
    our own.
Around the glistening
    wonder bent
The blue walls of the
    firmament,
No cloud above, no earth
    below,—
A universe of sky and
    snow!

JOHN GREENLEAF WHITTIER

Snow-Bound, 1866

A SLEIGHING SCENE NEAR BOSTON

SKATING ON JAMAICA POND, NEAR BOSTON

The tinkle of sleigh-bells on city streets
sounded a joyous note as both private sleighs and
public conveyances took to their runners

SLEIGHING SCENE ON BOSTON NECK

We are glad to present for our readers the spirited winter scene of one of the old landmarks of the city, a classic locality happily termed "Parnassus Corner" by noted essayist N. P. Willis. All our citizens will recognize it at once as the bookstore of Messrs. Ticknor & Fields, the well-known Athenian publishers. There are not many of these old buildings left, though fortunately Washington Street possesses some... How many changes we, who do not reckon many Olympiads, can recall in the city of our birth! How many fine old mansions razed! How many home sanctuaries profaned! It is very consoling, however, to reflect that this is all right, and that we are accomplishing our "manifest destiny"; and it is refreshing to know that if Washington Street, from Cornhill to School Street, has undergone many changes, it has not fallen into the hands of Goths and Vandals. On the contrary, it has become a Paternoster Row; it numbers its busy presses by the hundreds, and sends forth its books by the millions to gladden hands and hearts throughout our wide continent.

Ballou's Pictorial
February 21, 1857

ANCIENT BUILDING, CORNER OF SCHOOL AND WASHINGTON STREETS, BOSTON

Though it was hoped that Boston and its suburbs would soon be connected by the horse railway, doubts were expressed that such transit could ever enjoy a solid success because, as *Ballou's Pictorial,* June 7, 1856, said: "The founders of this village, never dreaming of its possible magnitude, were excessively economical in laying out the town throughfares, now too contracted for the vehicular tide which flows through them already." New York's broad and spacious streets were referred to with open envy. Boston's Tremont Street track had been laid experimentally; if the system did not work to the public satisfaction, the tracks were to be removed. Yet the obvious advantages of the horse cars were glowingly set forth: "Street surfaces are full of irregularities...passage over them in an ordinary conveyance reminds one of a run across a 'chop' sea. All this jolting is avoided on the rail. The cars glide as smoothly as a rowboat over a quiet stream." By 1857, Boston was making horse car fashion news with an open car on the Metropolitan Horse Railroad. The month was April; the car, "very pretty, with elaborate paintings," and the passengers' attire were well described:

THE NEW LOWELL RAILROAD DEPOT, CAUSEWAY STREET, BOSTON

TRAINS TAKING ENGINE FOR TRIP TO NEW YORK FROM BOSTON

The streets of Boston were among the first to bear steel tracks, in 1855, for newly organized urban transit by horse-drawn cars

THE BOSTON AND CAMBRIDGE NEW HORSE RAILROAD

"The new open car offers a very novel appearance as it moves through our streets filled with ladies and gentlemen, presenting a variety of costumes, black coats alternating with gaily colored silks and satins, collapsed frocks contrasting with expanded crinolines." Though the cars had been running for two years, each new one attracted crowds of onlookers along its routes.

The Metropolitan Horse Railroad—with 500 horses, about 50 open and top-seated cars, 50 omnibuses, and 80 closed and open sleighs—announced its intention to provide enough cars, each of which seated 24, for every passenger to have a seat. Added allurements were offices in the Metropolitan Hotel, "fitted up very liberally with a complete suite of apartments for the ladies, provided with all modern conveniences." So short a time before, people who lacked private carriages had been forced to walk, even to the suburbs. Then came the Omnibus "Hourly" on wheels or sleigh-runners according to season.

CLARENCE P. HORNUNG
Wheels Across America, 1959

THE METROPOLITAN HORSE RAILROAD, TREMONT STREET, BOSTON

Not long after the Pilgrims landed at Plymouth, Harvard started "in a small house in a cow-yard," the gift of a wealthy benefactor who endowed his estate for higher learning

But of course the heart of the University is the old College, and that lies to the north of the river, fenced in by the swirl and jangle of traffic which unfortunately makes Harvard Square one of the busiest arteries in the Greater Boston area. Here, however, withdrawn from all the noise and sick hurry of the day, the stranger may enter the Harvard Yard. Other American colleges have campuses, but Harvard has always had and always will have her Yard of grass and trees and youth and old familiar ghosts. There in the northwest corner, the oldest group of Harvard buildings links the fabulous past with the incredible present. These buildings are arranged, as the architectural fashion was, with "free form in Euclidean space." Massachusetts Hall, built at the public charge in 1720, has seen the nation and Harvard through ten wars. Designed as a residential hall, it quartered six hundred and forty soldiers during the Revolution. It was earlier the site of the first laboratory of experimental physics in America, and has served in turn as a dormitory, a theater workshop, and lately as an administration center, including the offices of the president. The original Harvard Hall was burned in 1764, but a new one was built in 1766. A lecture hall today, it, too, has in other centuries given various services: the college kitchen was there; so was the buttery; so was the Chapel. Just beyond Harvard Hall is the little gem of Georgian architecture called Holden Chapel, built in 1744, gift of the widow of a rich London merchant.

DAVID MC CORD

About Boston, 1975

HARVARD UNIVERSITY BUILDINGS

AUSTIN HALL, THE COLLEGE YARD, SEVER HALL, MEMORIAL HALL

A Cluster of Towns
Surrounds the Hub

WALTHAM ... BRIGHTON ... COHASSET ...

NAHANT ... ROXBURY ... MEDFORD ...

LONGWOOD ... BROOKLINE ... LOWELL ...

MANCHESTER ... SPRINGFIELD ... WORCESTER

... PROVINCETOWN ... PLYMOUTH ... LYNN

... NEW BEDFORD ... GLOUCESTER ...

ROCKPORT ... MARBLEHEAD

MAIN STREET, WALTHAM

A Cluster of Towns Surrounds the Hub

YOU NEED ONLY GLANCE AT A MAP of Massachusetts to appreciate the conglomeration of towns and villages that clusters around Boston. They sprang up on or near the dancing rivers, and a number are nearly as old as Boston itself. A few examples: Charlestown antedates Boston by a year; Arlington was founded in the same year as Boston (1630); Waltham followed in 1634; Brookline in 1638; Newton before 1640; Winchester in 1640; and Worcester in 1648.

Boston's city limits have expanded to include a number of cities and towns, some with traditions like those cherished by Boston. In a number of the surrounding towns, historic buildings are still well preserved. Charlestown, where the Battle of Bunker Hill was fought on June 17, 1775, is the site of a naval shipyard where the U.S.S. *Constitution* is moored.

Arlington is an important residential suburb with some interesting seventeenth-century buildings. The residential town and suburb of Brookline was a part of Boston known as "Muddy River," until it was separated in 1705. It was in Brookline that Amy Lowell made her home. Newton, west of Boston on the Charles River, is notable for its large number of handsome homes and several villages focused on industry. Here Nathaniel Hawthorne and Mary Baker Eddy had homes.

Roxbury and West Roxbury (with the Roxbury Latin School), Dorchester, Brighton, and Hyde Park are other towns that neighbor Boston and reflect its traditions.

Certain towns witnessed the early development of specific industries: Lowell for textiles, for example, and Roxbury for boots and shoes. Lowell, at the confluence of the Merrimack and Concord rivers, was settled in 1653. When its great mills were built in 1822, Lowell became one of the country's greatest textile centers.

Farmers in surrounding towns, attracted by the convenient and ready market, raised sheep for wool and hides; farmers' daughters welcomed the opportunity for gainful employment. The long hours—from six in the morning to six or seven in the evening—met with little objection: work on a farm was more strenuous and required even longer hours. To these girls, who had driven cattle to pasture, milked cows, worked in the fields, and scrubbed floors at home, mill work afforded an attractive alternative and tangible rewards.

Francis Cabot Lowell had made studies of conditions in English mills, and the mills at Lowell were regarded as models for their time.

Charles Dickens, who had visited the English mills and declared that the workers were living in deepest gloom, also visited Lowell on his American tour in 1842, and recorded his impressions in *American Notes.*

As the vast influx of foreign workers came to New England, conditions changed, and the labor force became predominantly Irish, followed by Greek, Polish, and Spanish.

It was in New England that organized industry began. Many of the settlers possessed crafts and skills gained from their English, Scottish, and Welsh backgrounds, which enabled them to start similar industries in Massachusetts. In *The Oxford History of the American People,* Samuel Eliot Morison writes:

> "Fullers from Rowley in Yorkshire set up a fulling mill in the Bay Colony, where home woven cloth could be shrunk and sheared. John Winthrop, Jr., later Governor of Connecticut, set up an ambitious and, for a time, a successful ironworks at Saugus, near Lynn. Here iron ore dug out of swamps and ponds, smelted with oak charcoal and flux from nearby rocks, was fashioned into pots and pans, anchors, chains, and other hardware for local needs."

Later, the men who ran the ironworks established others, and it is to these beginnings that the United States owes its stupendous iron and steel industry.

One evidence that the small towns shared the rich mental and spiritual resources that blessed Boston was to be found in the Reverend John Eliot. He lived in Roxbury and devised the first equivalent in Roman letters of the hitherto unwritten Algonquin language, making it possible for the entire Bible to be printed in Algonquin. This was the first Bible to be printed in the New World and its first translation into a "barbarous" language. (Another "first": the printing was done on the first press to be set up in the English colonies, in Harvard College Yard.)

Many of Boston's outlying towns—Chelsea, Revere, Somerville, Everett, Medford, Malden—are little different from Boston itself. A large percentage of their residents commute to jobs in Boston; others work in local factories. All these towns have a large admixture of first-generation Americans. Situated north and northwest of the hub, they have the closest ties to the city and are the most industrialized.

Less dominated by Boston, but well within its geographical area, are a number of old towns along the north shore and extending west to the valley of the Merrimack. These pursue their own existence, while enjoying the advantages of a proximity to Boston's culture and economy.

A distinctive aura seems to hover over Salem and Beverly, through tales of witch trials and histories of clipper captains and the fortunes made from voyages in the China trade.

Gloucester, though not in the Boston perimeter, remains a fishing port of great importance and is rimmed with fashionable summer resorts and private cottages.

Between the towns closest to Boston and those most distant, there are many small residential towns. A number of elegant suburbs encircle Beverly—towns like Wenham, Topsfield, Hamilton, and Manchester—where there are great estates, the homes of some of the wealthiest of Massachusetts families.

Only five miles from the heart of Boston, in the little town of Brighton, droves of cattle and sheep clogged the roads . . .

Brighton—originally a part of Cambridge—is five miles from Boston, and is one of the pleasantest towns in Massachusetts. Its natural boundary, the Charles River, provides a graceful and picturesque setting, affording lovely vistas from every angle. The chief interest in the town, at present, is in its celebrated Cattle Market, which originated during the Revolution, through the enterprise of Jonathan Winship, who bought cattle for the army; and thus from a limited trade, the market has become a very important feature of the business of the place. Sales for several years run to between two and three million dollars per annum, and the number of cattle to several hundred thousand. The importance of the market draws strangers from various parts of the country, and they are provided with comforts at the finest suburban hotel in the vicinity of Boston. This hotel is kept by Mr. Wilson, and stands in the first rank of "out-of-town" hotels. It is a pleasant summer resort, and thousands prove, by their frequent visits, its very great superiority to other hotels in the vicinity. Thursday is market day, and, for several days previous, the roads are thronged with droves of cattle and sheep. At one time, Brighton was the residence of Peter Faneuil, the donor of Faneuil Hall to the city of Boston.

Gleason's Pictorial Drawing-Room Companion, June 26, 1852

GOING TO BRIGHTON

WILSON'S HOTEL AT BRIGHTON

*. . . on their way to market and abattoir,
a reminder of the brisk livestock trade
dating back to Revolutionary times*

DRIVING TO MARKET

Boston became the great colonial market for live animals and meat. In 1663 the spot where the old state house stands was officially designated as a market place, and in 1742 Faneuil Hall became the gathering place for buyers and sellers. During or soon after the French and Italian War of 1756, Brighton sprang into prominence as a center for the cattle and meat trade, beginning with the activities of one butcher contractor, Jonathan Winship by name, who supplied the British army with meat. During the Revolution, Brighton continued its interest in the business and soon after the was over was the recognized market town in New England for cattle, hogs and sheep on the hoof, as well as for slaughtering and slaughter-house products. The Brighton Market was a magnified town fair held weekly. The peaceful village was for a day densely thronged with herds, drovers, and buyers. The trading done, Brighton reverted to its normal sleepy quiet. Brighton Market served as a model for many others, first in the east and afterward in the west; and Brighton itself continued to do a flourishing business until the growth of western packing houses killed most of its picturesque activities. To the present day, however, meat packing is one of its means of livelihood.

Pageant of America, 1926

CATTLE MARKET AT BRIGHTON

Seaside watering places attracted urban dwellers
by offering "every modern comfort": bathing cabanas,
and endless verandas for sea-gazing

It would be a curious and entertaining study to trace the evolution of our great hotels, from the cheerful roadside taverns and country inns, beloved of all travellers, to more pretentious road houses, to coffee houses, then to great crowded hotels. We could see the growth of these vast hotels, especially those of summer resorts, and also to their decay. In many fashionable watering-places great hotels have been torn down within a few years to furnish space for lawns and grounds around a splendid private residence. But the average American of means in the Northern states would spend a few weeks or even months at the big hotels at Saratoga, Niagara Falls, or the White Mountains. Along the Eastern coast, the chief resorts are to be found at Atlantic City, Old Point Comfort, and in New England, along Cape Cod and the environs of Boston.

ALICE MORSE EARLE
Stage Coach & Tavern
Days, 1900

ROCKLAND HOUSE, COHASSET

NAHANT HOTEL

*In nearby Roxbury and Medford, in addition to taverns
"affording entertainment and food for man and beast,"
modern hostelries were built that accommodated hundreds*

NORFOLK HOUSE, ROXBURY

As travel quickened—in 1826 Josiah Quincy, this time in a public stage, traveled from Boston to Washington in eight days—more specialized institutions took over the various functions of the tavern at key points on the road. Some served as tippling houses, some as boarding-houses, and others as hotels. In the larger cities where the concentration of travelers was greatest the city hotel burgeoned into a peculiarly American establishment where every need and convenience of the guest was anticipated, including many he was slow to recognize. Englishmen were astonished to learn that in some of these public places they could have their shirts washed and ironed while they bathed. The tinkling of ice was heard everywhere in every season of the year.

MARSHALL B. DAVIDSON
Life in America, 1951

FOUNTAIN HOUSE, MEDFORD

"Gentlemen's residences" and "elegant and tasteful private dwellings" appeared in the better and more quiet districts of the smaller towns . . .

We now present our readers with some accurately drawn views of gentlemen's residences in the adjoining city of Roxbury and the town of Brookline. They will revive pleasant memories among those familiar with the spots; they will also show the variety of tastes and styles exhibited in domestic architecture, and afford hints to those about to erect dwellings for themselves. In the variety of the examples shown are included cottages in the Elizabethan style of English architecture, those of Italian villa influence, the neo-Gothic style, the French chateau style and many others. It is evident that Americans have a wide choice of eclectic styles from which to choose when planning their residences.

Ballou's Pictorial
Drawing-Room Companion,
June 16, 1855

RESIDENCE AT ROXBURY

ITALIAN COTTAGE, ROXBURY

GENERAL WARREN HOUSE, ROXBURY

GOTHIC COTTAGE, HIGHLANDS

GOTHIC COTTAGE, ROXBURY

. . . displaying a composite of prevailing architectural styles, mostly of eclectic influence, then in vogue

In designing residential cottages, we have aimed rather at producing beauty by means of form and proportion, than by ornament; hence, it is not unlikely that those who have only a smattering of taste, and think a cottage cannot possess any beauty unless it is bedizened with ornaments, will be disappointed with the simplicity of most of these plans. But we trust, on the other hand, that persons of more information and more correct taste, and especially those who have followed us in our development of the true sources of interest in rural architecture, will agree with us that tasteful simplicity, not fanciful complexity, is the true character for cottages.

A.J. DOWNING

The Architecture of Country Houses, 1850

CARNES' VILLA, HIGHLANDS

RESIDENCE AT LONGWOOD, BROOKLINE

HOUSE AT LONGWOOD

GOTHIC COTTAGE, LONGWOOD

COTTAGE AT LONGWOOD

By dam and millrace, the swift-flowing rivers gave motive power to New England's rapidly growing textile industry . . .

We were thus entering the State of New Hampshire on the bosom of the flood formed by the tribute of its innumerable valleys. The river was the only key which could unlock its maze, presenting its hills and valleys, its lakes and streams, in their natural order and position. The Merrimack, or Sturgeon River, is formed by the confluence of the Pemigewasset, which rises near the Notch of the White Mountains, and the Winnepisiogee, which drains the lake of the same name, signifying "The Smile of the Great Spirit." From their junction it runs south seventy-eight miles to Massachusetts, and thence east thirty-five miles to the sea. I have traced its stream from where it bubbles out of the rocks of the White Mountains above the clouds, to where it is lost amid the salt billows of the ocean on Plum Island beach. At first it comes on murmuring to itself by the base of stately and retired mountains, through moist primitive woods whose juices it receives, where the bear still drinks it, and the cabins of settlers are far between, and there are few to cross its stream; enjoying in solitude its cascades still unknown to fame; by long ranges of mountains of Sandwich and Squam, slumbering like tumuli of Titans, with the peaks of Mossehillock, the Haystack, and Kearsarge reflected in its waters; where the maple and the raspberry, those lovers of the hills, flourish amid temperate dews.

HENRY DAVID THOREAU

A Week on the Concord and Merrimack Rivers, 1852

JUNCTION OF THE CONCORD AND MERRIMACK RIVERS, LOWELL

MERRIMACK STREET, LOWELL

. . . where the hum of shuttle, loom, and bobbin meant work for willing hands and the creation of a new labor force—the "Lowell girls"

MANCHESTER PRINT WORKS, MANCHESTER, N.H.

Each new mill erected by the Associates copied Francis Lowell's boarding house plan. While the number of girls in all boarding house mills were never a majority of the employees in cotton textiles, the Lowell girls became far more famous than any other group. Foreign visitors regarded Lowell as one of the sights that must not be missed, and famous Americans lectured there to audiences composed mainly of mill girls. For daughters of back country New England farmers, the mills of Lowell were a finishing school or college where they could learn the ways of the world and make money in the process. The companies made the change from farm to factory easy by sending agents in long black covered wagons to explain the rules to hesitant parents, and to bring the girls and their baggage direct to the boarding houses. No doubt the agents talked more of lectures and libraries, clothes and smart shops than of the twelve to thirteen-hour work day. Or they held out the goal of four dollars a week, two dollars and seventy-five cents more than the cost of board, without mentioning that few girls ever worked fast enough to achieve such pay. But to girls used to hard work on poor farms, to big families in little houses, the realities were not too bad. Six girls sleeping in a small room might seem crowded to an upper class visitor, but to the girls it was just like home.

T.C. COCHRAN

The Factory Comes to New England

BOOTT COTTON MILLS, LOWELL

On the important east-west turnpike from Boston to Albany, in the state's midlands, Springfield developed into a diversified industrial center . . .

Establishment of the United States Armory at Springfield in 1777 set in motion a beginning of industry. Pittsfield had a woolen mill by 1801. The establishment of Williams College in 1793 and Amherst College in 1821 began to provide trained leadership for a new generation. Stimulated in the beginning by the British blockade, by 1825 more than twenty turnpike corporations and an equal number of bridge-building companies were hard at work surveying and building east-west highways to carry regular stagecoach service from Boston to Albany. In 1839 a new steam railroad began to provide service between Worcester and Springfield, and by 1855 western Massachusetts was covered by a network of fifteen railroads, letting inhabitants out from behind their mountain barriers and letting summer visitors in. Still more important, freight traffic now made possible a full participation of these western counties in the burgeoning industrial revolution, that rapidly made of the Springfield-Westfield-Holyoke-Chicopee area an industrial complex rivaling those of Fall River-New Bedford, Lawrence-Haverhill, and the Greater Boston region. Springfield's population grew to 10,000 by 1840, and its textile, paper and machinery factories soon mushroomed into the expanding cities of Westfield, Chicopee and Holyoke, to produce an industrial region today populated by almost 300,000 people.

HENRY F. HOWE

Massachusetts,

There She Is—Behold Her

1960

COURT HOUSE, SPRINGFIELD

SPRINGFIELD, FROM THE LONGMEADOW ROAD

. . . as the first steam railroad, in 1839, extended service to new areas around Worcester and previously isolated villages

STATE INSTITUTION, WORCESTER

You have seen, I think, W---, the distant village in New England, where I spent nearly the last half of the last century. Perhaps, however, you have merely looked at it as a passing traveller, and did not remark its simple beauty. To memory, every tree, every green pasture and humble dwelling, are as familiar as the room I sit in. It was distant about two miles from the ocean, and scattered on both sides of a small but tranquil and beautiful river, which was crossed by a wooden bridge in the centre of the village. On the north side rose gentle hills gracefully from the river, and on the south spread out level meadows, dotted with buttonwood trees and weeping elms. The meeting-house and parsonage were on the north side, overlooking on the south the village, whose houses were scattered about the bridge, and ascended, at least the better sort, towards the church. Beyond the hills on the north, stretched out, as if to shelter us, the protecting forest. The meeting-house was the square, barn-like structure, common at that period to all New England. Ours, however, was adorned with a steeple and belfry, and graced with a most sweet sounding bell.

ELIZA BUCKMINSTER LEE
Sketches of a New England Village, c. 1850

LINCOLN SQUARE, WORCESTER

Due south of Boston lies New Bedford, on a well-protected harbor that accounted for more whale fishing than any other American port on the Atlantic coast . . .

In the latter half of the century more than a third of the nation's woolens were produced in Massachusetts. Fall River, Lawrence, Lowell, and New Bedford led all other cities in cotton manufacture. By 1890 Lawrence was third and Lowell fourth among American cities in the manufacture of woolens. By 1900 Massachusetts produced almost half the shoes in the United States, a quarter of these coming from Lynn, and large fractions from Brockton, Haverhill, Marlborough and Worcester. Shoe machinery from Beverly, Boston and Waltham and paper-mill machinery from Lowell, Pittsfield, Lawrence and Worcester were world-famous. All this prodigious and bustling prosperity rested, once the machines had been built and paid for, on the shifting base of a labor surplus provided by unceasing immigration through Boston's port, which remained a good immigrant port because it also furnished the shortest commercially practical route for sending the British mails to Canada.

HENRY F. HOWE
Massachusetts,
There She Is—Behold Her
1960

COURT HOUSE, NEW BEDFORD

CITY HALL, NEW BEDFORD

*. . . while to the north lies Lynn, a coastal city
whose origins may be traced to its early tanneries
and their subsequent growth into a great shoe industry*

THE EXCHANGE, LYNN

THE COMMON, LYNN

ATLANTIC BEACH, LYNN

The town of Lynn, first settled in 1629 and incorporated the following year, was originally called by its Indian name, Saugus. By 1850 it became a city with a population of over 13,000. Lynn's first inhabitants were farmers, but gradually they turned their attention to the manufacture of ladies' shoes, which flourished to become the city's principal business. The stock for the shoes is cut in larger buildings; the uppers are tied in bundles and given to females to be bound at home. They are then returned to the manufactories where they are sewn to the soles by men. The shoe workmen are called cordwainers, more properly cordovaniers; the word being derived from Cordovan leather, originally made in Cordoba, Spain from goat skins brought over from Morocco, in Africa. When the shoes are finished, they are packed in large wooden crates, sixty to a box. It is estimated that there are about 150 factories, employing 10,000, more than half of whom are females. In addition to Lynn's major shoe industry, there are vessels engaged in whaling, cod and mackerel fishing and coastwise shipping.

*Ballou's Pictorial
Drawing-Room Companion,
January 10, 1857*

On Cape Ann, in Gloucester and Rockport, fishing was the grim business of men who ventured to "go down to the sea in ships" . . .

Then up and spoke the orator of the occasion, another pillar of the municipality, bidding the world welcome to Gloucester, and incidentally pointing out wherein Gloucester excelled the rest of the world. Then he turned to the sea-wealth of the city, and spoke of the price that must be paid for the yearly harvest. They would hear later the names of their lost dead—one hundred and seventeen of them. (The widows stared a little, and looked at one another here.) Gloucester could not boast any overwhelming mills or factories. Her sons worked for such wage as the sea gave; and they all knew that neither Georges nor the Banks were cowpastures. The utmost that folk ashore could accomplish was to help the widows and the orphans; and after a few general remarks he took this opportunity of thanking, in the name of the city, those who had so public-spiritedly consented to participate in the exercises of the occasion.

RUDYARD KIPLING
*For Those in Peril on
the Sea*

GLOUCESTER AND ROCKPORT

. . . reminding us, as have many poets, that tragedy always lurks in New England's "stern and rock-bound coast"

SWALLOWS' CAVE, NAHANT

In the hush of the autumn night
I hear the voice of the sea,
In the hush of the autumn night
It seems to say to me—
Mine are the winds above,
Mine are the caves below,
Mine are the dead of yesterday
And the dead of long ago!

And I think of the fleet that sailed
From the lovely Gloucester shore,
I think of the fleet that sailed
And came back nevermore;
My eyes are filled with tears,
And my heart is numb with woe—
It seems as if 'twere yesterday,
And it all was long ago!

THOMAS BAILEY ALDRICH
The Voice of the Sea, 1907

NORMAN'S WOE, GLOUCESTER

Colder and louder blew the wind,
  A gale from the Northeast,
The snow fell hissing in the brine,
  And the billows frothed like yeast.

Down came the storm, and smote amain
  The vessel in its strength;
She shuddered and paused, like a frighted steed,
  Then leaped her cable's length....

Such was the wreck of the Hesperus,
  In the midnight and the snow!
Christ save us all from a death like this,
  On the reef of Norman's Woe!

HENRY WADSWORTH LONGFELLOW
The Wreck of the Hesperus, 1839

Marblehead's first settlers were hard-bitten fishermen from Britain's Cornwall who, in 1629, "came not for religion but to catch fish"

Just before reaching Salem one is called off by the lure of Marblehead. Wonderful old houses remain here, there being at least three or four of great distinction which are all available for examination. The bay of Marblehead is a gem of beauty and one who loves at once natural scenery and old America finds them both in this town at their best. One is here away from the bustle of the city, yet by no means distant from the attractive features of American outdoor life. Marblehead is a yachting center; its harbor gay with snowy winged craft; its streets uneven, winding, full of surprises, and its back country appealing from its variety of roadsides.

WALLACE NUTTING
Massachusetts Beautiful
1923

TOWN HALL, MARBLEHEAD

MARBLEHEAD AND HARBOR

A glimpse of the harbor appears between weather-beaten houses that shoulder one another, on narrow streets and winding lanes

CURING FISH

Tribute needs to be paid to the fishing industry, which was the perpetual work horse that kept the other enterprises going. In good years such ports as Gloucester, Wellfleet, Hingham and Cohasset each packed more than 40,000 barrels of mackerel. Four or five voyages were commonly made each summer following the mackerel northward as their "schools" migrated. Often the first voyage in May found mackerel off Cape May, New Jersey, and a June voyage off Block Island. The midsummer voyages were short, in New England waters, but fall frequently found the schooners traveling as far as Bay of St. Lawrence. In port, the wharves were busy as the already split, gibbed and salted fish were packed in barrels by boys in their early teens at 25 cents per day. Local cooper shops made the barrels, and local saltworks evaporated much of the salt from sea water. Each schooner had a crew of about ten men and boys. Originally these were all New England born: by mid-century a considerable immigration of Portuguese seamen were prospering in the fishing trade, many of them becoming masters of schooners with the encouragement of Yankee owners.

HENRY F. HOWE
Massachusetts, There She Is—Behold Her, 1960

WEIGHING FISH

MARBLEHEAD SCHOONER

GLOUCESTER HARBOR

*At the northern tip of Cape Cod's hook stands Provincetown
—across the bay from Plymouth, where the* Mayflower's *Pilgrims
landed, in 1620, to establish the Massachusetts Bay Colony*

Cape Cod wears its heart on its sleeve; and wears it like a Christian on the very end of its sleeve in lieu of a fist. For where the arm of earth gathers protectingly about Cape Cod Bay, and its fingers enfold a harbor of a thousand ships, there is concentrated in a league of shore, village and dune the quintessence of the Cape's beauty and romance and dear, naive humanity. Provincetown is the natural climax of the Cape. You work up to this climax from Plymouth, past the quaint town halls, meeting-houses, fan-light portals, water-mills and wind-mills of places with such well-flavored names as Sandwich (where the Cape proper begins), Barnstable, Hyannis, Yarmouth, Harwich, Chatham, Well-fleet and Truro. You cross wide-swelling uplands from which you may look down, as at a map modeled in relief, upon the curve of the Cape's gold and green and wine-red arm, and see how the stacklike towers of the wireless station are like a bit of Pittsburgh that has strayed by accident to spotless climes; and notice how the sand-spit out toward Provincetown gleams like a horizontal exclamation point of gold.

ROBERT HAVEN SCHAUFFLER
Romantic America, 1913

PLYMOUTH, FROM THE BURYING GROUND

PROVINCETOWN HARBOR

High Peaks & Highlights in Scenic New Hampshire

SHELBURNE FALLS . . . MOUNT WASHINGTON . . .

COG WHEEL RAILROAD . . . GORHAM . . .

DIXVILLE NOTCH . . . CONCORD . . .

HILLSBOROUGH . . . LAKE WINNIPESAUKEE

. . . PORTSMOUTH . . . MEREDITH BRIDGE

SHELBURNE FALLS

High Peaks & Highlights in Scenic New Hampshire

ITS LAND AREA IS MODEST, ITS AGRICUL--
tural terrain limited; but its mountains
are magnificent, its water courses
tumultous and beautiful, and its lakes
numerous and of an incredible loveliness. The
White Mountains of New Hampshire are the
highest in New England and —excepting only
the Black Mountains of North Carolina—the
highest east of the Mississippi. With the Pro-
vince of Quebec as its northern boundary, the
Connecticut River defining its western border,
Massachusetts on the south, and Connecticut
on the east—New Hampshire has just 18 miles
of shoreline on the Atlantic Ocean. Its largest
lake, the Winnipesaukee, has an almost incredible number of habitable islands—274—in
its 44,000 acres of silvery waters. The White
Mountains form a great plateau, with a score
of peaks of various heights, traversed by deep,
narrow valleys. In the branches of the Connecticut River valley are the Androscoggin, Saco,
and Pemigewasset rivers. Countless little
streams dance down steep glens from mountain springs, forming waterfalls and pathways.

"Starting from Centre Harbor, a summer resort of considerable celebrity...the reglar stagecoach for Conway and the mountains is soon among high hills...winding in and out among them, the stage passes now under the dark, frowning brow of a cliff, and afterward by some deep ravine, and then comes upon a lofty plateau... till at Eaton the summit of Mount Washington is often distinctly seen....Driving on the mountain road...one watches the great hill-tops come up, like billows, one after another, from the sea of mountains round out, as the coach winds and twists among them....Not only the mountains, but the village itself, and the gentle meadows of the Saco, add to the soft charm of this very Arcadia of the White Hills." wrote Susan N. Carter, in *Picturesque America.*

Historic Portsmouth—New Hampshire's only seaport—with flagstone streets and gracious homes dating from the great whaling days, is located on an estuary of the Pistaguu, at Salmon Hills. The state's abundance of streams and lakes has been extensively harnessed, manufacturing being concentrated in the lower valleys of the Connecticut and the Merrimack Rivers. Manchester, Nashua, Concord, and Keene are the largest cities. While the ocean tempers the coastal climate, the inland areas are subject to great extremes—with as much as eight feet of snowfall in the mountains.

The rocky topography and stony soil prohibit commercial agriculture, but second-growth fir, spruce, and hardwoods cover much of the land, making lumber, pulp, and paper important industries, especially in the north. Poultry and poultry products, and livestock, apples, and nursery and dairy products are the chief sources of farm income.

Although New Hampshire is known as the Granite State, granite is no longer extensively quarried. Leather and leather products are important industries in the southern part of the state, in addition to the manufacture of textiles, electrical equipment, and machinery. New Hampshire is noted for its efforts to revive native crafts: pottery-making, weaving, wood carving; and it is the site of two Shaker communities, famous for their handcrafted furniture and home accessories.

From the early 19th century, the resort and vacation-related industry has been a primary source of income. The cog railway held great fascination for tourists in the early 1870s, ascending into the clouds, to the top of Mount Washington. The railway was scarcely less a feat of engineering than a test of patience, for the New Hampshire legislature was highly scornful of the plan, and the short summer season, while it was a-building reduced working days to a minimum.

With the largest legislature of any government in the world, numbering 443, every local community in New Hampshire has its own representatives. Martin Pring (1605) and Captain John Smith (1614) gave the first accounts of the region now known as New Hampshire. The Council of New England—successors to the Plymouth Colony—issued a Royal Grant. Settlements were made and abandoned, until a group of Anglican farmers and fishermen founded Portsmouth in 1630. Massachusetts annexed south New Hampshire in 1641, claiming misrepresentation. By 1679, New Hampshire was proclaimed a royal colony, with appointees of the Crown in authority. It was only in 1741 that one man, Benning Wentworth, became governor exclusively for New Hampshire. The French and Indian War had prevented colonization in the inland areas but, as Indian hostility lessened, a land rush started. Lumber camps were set up and sawmills were built along the streams. When the king's deputies blazed the tall white pines with arrows, to mark them for the Royal Navy, much resentment was aroused. As the American Revolution started, many in the populace were eager for independence. A committee of safety was organized, and it is claimed that the Sons of Liberty in Portsmouth raised the first liberty pole in the colonies. The people met on January 3, 1776, and formed a new government, with a legislature, council, and governor (called the president).

New Hampshire's beauty and serenity have long attracted artists and writers. Hawthorne, Whittier, and Longfellow spent summers here. Thomas Bailey Aldrich was a native of the state. In the work of Robert Frost, the poet's own words declare that there is not one of his poems "but has something in it of New Hampshire."

On one wintry occasion, as we are told in Drake's *Heart of the White Mountains,* the wind rose to such a fury that the inmates of the station, expecting every moment that the building would be blown over, wrapped themselves in blankets and quilts, binding them tightly with ropes, to which were attached bars of iron, so that, as one of the men said in relating the story, "if the house went by the board, we might stand a chance—a slim one—of anchoring somewhere, somehow."...

...But had the house gone, they would probably have been lifted from their feet like bags of wool, "dashed against the rocks, and smashed like eggshells," as one of the men coolly remarked to his visitor.

Harper's Weekly
January 14, 1882

CARRIAGE ROAD, MOUNT WASHINGTON

PANORAMA OF THE WHITE MOUNTAINS

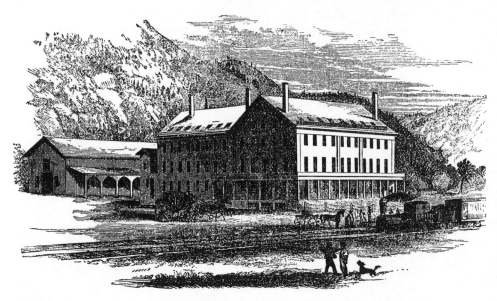

ALPINE HOUSE, GORHAM

METEOROLOGICAL STATION, MT. WASHINGTON

Long before the Civil War, thousands of vacationers braved the rigors of mountain climbing to enjoy the scenic beauties celebrated by poets and painters . . .

FOOT OF THE MOUNTAIN

MOUNT WASHINGTON RAILROAD

The road is really as steep in some places as a flight of stairs...But we think of the atmospheric brakes, of the friction brakes, of the ratchet wheel, and the cogs...The stoutest of the party looks a little pale; but we feel the firm grip of cog upon cog; we remember that the wheel is so clamped upon the pin-rigged middle rail that neither the engine nor the car can be lifted or thrown off; that the pawl that dropped into the ratchet-wheel would hold us in the steepest place; that the shutting of a valve... in the atmospheric brakes effectually stops the wheels from turning...We seem to go up from the middle of a great valley; there are no level places. The mountains about us shrink into small hills. Now, no trees. Now, only rocks. Now, we are at the top, cloud-wrapped.

Harper's Weekly
August 21, 1869

JACOB'S LADDER

Not any drift boulders in Green and White Mountains, because the old ice-sheet plucked them from these mountains and dropped them over the landscape to the south; here they lie like a herd of slumbering elephants with their calves, sleeping the sleep of geologic ages. The view of the White Mountains very impressive. We came through the Crawford Notch, down and down and down, over a superb road, through woods, with these great rocky peaks shouldering the sky on each side. Simply stupendous!

JOHN BURROUGHS

TIP-TOP HOUSE

AMONG THE CLOUDS

The state's capital at Concord, on both sides of the Merrimack, where as early as 1818 its famed Concord coaches were shipped throughout the world

If I must choose which I
would elevate—
The people or the already
lofty mountains,
I'd elevate the already
lofty mountains.
The only fault I find with
old New Hampshire
Is that her mountains
aren't quite high
enough.
I was not always so;
I've come to be so.
How, to my sorrow, how
have I attained
A height from which to
look down critical
On mountains? What has
given me assurance
To say what height
becomes New Hamp-
shire mountains,
Or any mountains? Can it
be some strength
I feel as of an earthquake
in my back
To heave them higher to
the morning star?

ROBERT FROST

TOWN OF CONCORD

BIRTHPLACE OF PRESIDENT PIERCE, HILLSBOROUGH

Lake Winnipesaukee, so named by the Indians, means "Smile of the Great Spirit." One of the largest lakes, boasts 183 miles of shoreline and 274 islands

RED HILL FROM LAKE WINNIPESAUKEE

One of the most travelled routes to the White Mountains is by railroad to Concord, and thence to Lake Winnipesaukee (pronounced by the Indians Win-ne-pe-sock-e, with the accent on the penultima), an excellent point of departure for the mountain region. It signifies the poetical feeling of the aborigines, and their appreciation of the beauties of nature. No one who has lingered by the magnificent shores of this sheet of water, who has gazed upon its broad expanse dotted with numerous islands, and gleaming in the rays of the rising and setting sun, will deny the appropriateness of the Indian name...

...The lake stretches into seven large bays, three on the west, three on the east, and one on the north. Its waters are of crystalline purity, and its depth in some places is said to be unfathomable. The islets that gem its bosom are said to number three hundred and sixty-five, the largest of them containing five hundred acres of fertile soil, yielding heavy crops of corn and grain.

Ballou's Pictorial Drawing-Room Companion
June 12, 1855

LAKE WINNIPESAUKEE

CENTER HARBOR, LAKE WINNIPESAUKEE

First settled in 1623, early Portsmouth grew rapidly from interests in fishing, shipbuilding, and privateering, but settled down to enjoy the glory of its naval shipyard

The town of Portsmouth, N.H., the state's only seaport on a short strip of Atlantic coast, is located on the south side of the Piscataqua River, three miles inland from the sea. Its defense built to protect both the town and its historic naval base are Fort Constitution and Fort Mc-Clary, the latter in Kittery, opposite. It was here on Navy Island that the *North America,* the first line-of-battle ship was launched, during the Revolution. Portsmouth has long been proud of the skill of its naval architects and builders. Machine shops, iron foundries and saw mills are manned by highly skilled craftsmen for which the town is celebrated. In 1850 the population of Portsmouth was nearly ten thousand.

UNITED STATES NAVY YARD, PORTSMOUTH

Gleason's Pictorial   July 23, 1853

MARKET SQUARE, PORTSMOUTH

Meredith is situated in the center of the state between lakes Winnipesaukee and Waukewan, a region noted for exquisite lake and mountain scenery

PORTSMOUTH, FROM THE NORTH

Gleason's Pictorial   October 30, 1852

Meredith Bridge is located in the neighborhood of exquisite lakes, studded throughout with small green islands, burdened with rich foliage and surrounded with lofty mountains on every side. The fertility of its soil and the general wholesomeness of the area form the nucleus of attraction which gives the town preference for its annual agricultural fair under state auspices. The many huge tents erected within the grounds provide ample space for the exhibition of farm implements, machinery and fancy articles of every description. The judging of horses, cattle and hogs culminates in keen competition from entries from all corners of the Granite State.

NEW HAMPSHIRE STATE FAIR, MEREDITH BRIDGE

The Granite State—noted for the grandeur of its mountains —has but a tiny outlet to the sea, where the New England coastline continues with its jagged, rocky formations

Unafraid, too, we watched the summer tempests, and listened to the deep, melodious thunder rolling away over the rain-calmed ocean. It was fine indeed from the lighthouse itself to watch the storm come rushing over the sea and ingulf us in our helplessness. How the rain weltered down over the great panes of plate glass,—floods of sweet, fresh water that poured off the rocks and mingled with the bitter brine. I wondered why the fresh floods never made the salt sea any sweeter. Those pale flames that we beheld burning from the spikes of the lightning-rod, I suppose were identical with the St. Elmo's fire that I have seen seen described as haunting the spars of ships in thunder-storms. And here I am reminded of a story told by some gentlemen visiting Appledore sixteen or eighteen years ago. They started from Portsmouth for the Shoals in a whaleboat, one evening in summer, with a native Star-Islander, Richard Randall by name, to manage the boat. They had sailed about half the distance, when they were surprised at seeing a large ball of fire, like a rising moon, rolling toward them over the sea from the south.

CELIA THAXTER

Among the Isles of Shoals, 1873

ALONG NEW HAMPSHIRE'S ATLANTIC SHORES

Amid Vermont's
Green Hills

LAKE MEMPHREMAGOG . . . MOUNT

MANSFIELD . . . CORDUROY ROAD . . .

GREEN MOUNTAINS . . . SMUGGLER'S

NOTCH . . . MONTPELIER . . . SUGAR

MAPLE HARVEST . . . ON THE

MISSISQUOI RIVER . . . MARBLE QUARRIES,

WEST RUTLAND . . . PROCTOR

OWL'S HEAD LANDING, LAKE MEMPHREMAGOG

Amid Vermont's Green Hills

VERMONT'S GENTLE, GREEN-covered hills conceal a granite foundation, resembling the stern, rocklike character of its natives. *Vert:* green; *mont:* mountain; so the state reveals the source of its name. Samuel de Champlain is the first white man known to have reached the area. He had laid the founda-tions for Quebec and then, in 1609, journeyed south with a Huron war party to the beautiful lake that now bears his name. Not until 1724 was the first permanent settlement built near what is now Brattleboro. In 1741, the commis-sion of the Royal Governor of New Hamp-shire, Benning Wentworth, declared New Hampshire's boundary to extend across the

Merrimack, "until it met with our [i.e., the king's] other governments"—the eastern limits of the colony of New York. Violent disputes erupted, but New York's claim, to what is now Vermont, was upheld by the British.

The Revolution brought border battles to a temporary halt. In 1777, Vermont declared itself an independent state, but due to New York's opposition the Continental Congress refused to give Vermont recognition as a colony or state. Vermonters reaffirmed their independence and adopted a constitution. For ten years after the American victory at Yorktown, Vermont remained an independent state, performed all the services of a sovereign government, coined money, established post offices, naturalized citizens, and appointed ambassadors to foreign countries. In 1791, Vermont entered the Union.

Limited arable land and abundant rainfall make grazing a major industry, and the famous breed of Morgan horse was developed here. Hay is the state's chief crop. Dairy farming dominates agriculture, and milk is shipped in great quantities to the metropolitan markets of Boston and New York.

John Gunther, in *Inside America,* tells us: "Vermont has smooth and gentle dulcet hills—yes, but underneath is slate, marble, granite. This granite is solid in the state character. ...The triumph of Vermont is a certain richness of character—richness that is nevertheless stern. The typical Vermonter is rugged, reticent, suspicious of outsiders, frugal, individualistic, and with great will to survive....

"The basis of life in Vermont remains agriculture; this in turn is based on fluid milk. Most Vermont dairy farms are small, worked by their own owners, and held in the same family for generations. The farmers are well organized; most belong to the Grange. ...Though the typical Vermont farmer may be poor, he will go through almost any hardship to educate his children."

Vermont, said to have more cattle than people, is also known for maple syrup, apples, and potatoes. In Rutland and Proctor, industry is concentrated on the quarrying and finishing of marble; in Barre, Vermont's famous granite is quarried and processed. From the self-sufficient farms of pioneer days, Vermont agriculture developed commercially to beef cattle and grain. When the growth of the West supplied these at lower prices, and wool textile mills sprang up in New England, Vermont farmers turned to sheep-raising. After the Civil War, with competition from west Australia and South America, farmers turned to an easier life in the cities or migrated west. Abandoned farms became a common sight but, through a transition to dairy farming, Vermont's agriculture was saved from a permanent decline.

The most truly rural of the New England states, Vermont lies between the granite masses of the White Mountains on one side, and the Adirondacks on the other. Its soil is mellower than its neighbors; its water courses gentler. Forested Green Mountains traverse the state from north to south in four groups: the Green Mountains (proper), from Canada to the Massachusetts line, rising to Mount Mansfield which is Vermont's highest peak; the Taconic Mountains, an important source of marble; the Granite Hills, named for their valuable stone; and the Sandrock Hills. There are also scattered hills, called monadnocks.

Crawford's Notch in the White Mountains and Smugglers' Notch in the Green Mountains would be called canyons in the far West. Although the Eastern notches are not so ruggedly grand, they are more beautiful. Mosses and ferns cover them, and, in some places, ancient roots twine around the rocks like boa-constrictors. Huge gnarled roots encircle the rocks like giant anacondas. Abundant moisture has led to the luxuriant growth of lichens and ferns and has painted the rocks with delicate tints.

The unspoiled beauty of quiet towns and wooded mountains draws many thousands of vacationers each year; and climbers and hikers are attracted to the Long Trail,—which runs along the Green Mountains the entire length of the state—to make tourism a leading industry and major source of state income.

The serene Vermont countryside—intricately interlaced with soft mountain slopes, tilled fields, and gentle brooks—suddenly erupts in its Green Mountains . . .

ROCK OF TERROR

Mount Mansfield, the highest of the Green Mountain range, is situated near the northern extremity, about twenty miles, in a direct line east, or a little north of east, from Burlington, on Lake Champlain. This mountain has been less popular among tourists and pleasure seekers than the White Mountains and the Catskills principally because its attractions have been little known. Of recent years, it has been more visited than formerly; and a good hotel at Stowe, five miles from its base, has now every summer its throng of tourists. There is also a Summit House, situated at the base of the highest peak known as the Nose, where travellers may find plain but suitable accommodation if they wish to prolong their stay on the mountain top overnight. Mansfield is conveniently reached by rail from Burlington; and thence by Concord coaches ten miles to Stowe. From Stowe a carriage road reaches to the summit of the mountain. . . This mountain is, moreover, not without the usual number of faces and resemblances to familiar objects, among the most notable of which is that described as the "Old Woman of the Mountain," represented herewith.

ROSSITER JOHNSON
Picturesque America, 1872

VIEW FROM MOUNTAIN ROAD

. . . where, in granite boulders, sharp cliffs,
and forest-clad escarpments, Nature sculpts
her time-worn shapes and forms

Vermont is, and perhaps ever will be, the most purely rural of all the older States. Though bordered by Lake Champlain, and pretty well supplied with railways, she seems to be aside from any great thoroughfare, and to hold her greenness nearly unsoiled by the dust of travel and traffic. Between the unyielding granite masses of the White Mountains on the one side, and the Adirondack Wilderness on the other, lies this happy valley of simple contentment, with its mellower soil and gentler water-courses, its thriftier farmers and more numerous herds, its marbleledges, its fertile uplands, and its own mountains of gentler slope and softened outline. Nearly through the middle runs the Green Mountain range, giving rise to a thousand murmuring rivulets and modest rivers, that lapse down through green-browed hills and crumbling limestone cliffs and sunny meadow lands, now turned quickly by a mossy ledge, and now skirting a bit of native forest, until they lose themselves on the one side in the deep-channelled Connecticut, or on the other in the historic waters of Lake Champlain.

ROSSITER JOHNSON

Picturesque America, 1872

CORDUROY BRIDGE,
MOUNT MANSFIELD ROAD

THE OLD WOMAN OF THE MOUNTAIN

At Smuggler's Notch, "giant trees find nourishment in crevices, and huge, gnarled roots encircle the rocks like immense anacondas"

Another view shows us the mountain cliffs looming through the mists of what is known as Smuggler's Notch. In the far West this notch would be called a canyon, but it differs mainly from the canyons of the Sierra in being more picturesque—not so ruggedly grand as those rocky walls, but the abundant moisture has filled it with superb forest growths, has covered all the rocks with ferns and lichens, has painted the stone with delicious tints. The sides of the Notch rise to an altitude of about a thousand feet, the upper verge of the cliffs rising above the fringe of mountain trees that cling to their sides. The floor of the Notch is covered with immense boulders and fallen masses of rocks, which in this half-lighted vault have partly crumbled, and given foothold for vegetation. Mosses and ferns cover them, and in many instances great trees have found nourishment in the crevices, sometimes huge gnarled roots encircling the rocks like immense anacondas. Smuggler's Notch has a hundred poetical charms that deserve for it a better name. It is so called because once used as a hiding place for goods smuggled over the Canada border.

ROSSITER JOHNSON

Picturesque America, 1872

VIEW TOWARD SMUGGLER'S NOTCH

Vermont's vast Lake Memphremagog, most of which projects into bordering Canada, affords vistas of striking beauty from every perspective

LAKE MEMPHREMAGOG, NORTH FROM OWL'S HEAD

We are fast nearing Owl's Head. The boat winds in and out between the cedar-robed islands, and the golden haze vanishes into the clear and breezy day. We do not land during the journey down the lake, but pass Owl's Head, with only a glimpse of its magnificent height. At one place the shore is almost perpendicular, and on the southern side there is an extraordinary granite boulder, balanced on a natural pedestal, named Balance Rock. Hereabout, too, are the villas of some wealthy Montreal merchants, enclosed in magnificent parks on the banks. Owl's Head is the most prominent mountain, and is cone-shaped. But in our passage to the head of the lake, we see other heights that do not fall far below it. Here is Mount Elephantus, now faintly resembling an elephant's back, afterward changing, as we proceed further north, into a horseshoe form. In the morning we ascend Owl's Head. The pathway from the hotel is in good condition, overarched by pines and cedars, bordered by pleasant fields. The air is filled with the fragrance of wild flowers, mosses and ferns. Occasionally, through the green curtain that shelters us from the mounting sun, we catch a glimpse of the untroubled, azure sky. The summit reached, we have such a view as rewards our toil. Looking south, we see the lake from end to end, its island and villages, the near rivers flashing in the sunlight.

W.H. RIDEING

Picturesque America, 1872

At maple-sugar time, Vermonters get out their giant kettles and sap yokes to harvest maple sugar, at one time their sole sweetener

At this season of the year sugar orchards become places of much resort, especially for those who love the sweet things of life. In this village parties are frequently formed, who take a trip to some maple orchard in the vicinity, and there regale their palates with maple molasses. These maple sugar manufactories are generally located in romantic spots—in some beautiful valley or on some delightful hillside, where the air is pure and invigorating, and the landscape views enchanting and picturesque. Vermont contains thousands of such delightful retreats; and at this season of the year, when the crystal waters of the brooks are released from their frozen bands and come leaping down the mountain sides, waking the beautiful trout from his winter's sleep, and filling the valleys and groves with sweet music, it is pleasant to visit these sugar orchards, drink sap, lap maple molasses, and make love! Let the Vermont ladies beware; for in such places they may fall in love, while they would not dream of such a thing in their homes.

A BURLINGTON
CORRESPONDENT
The Boston Atlas, 1852

SUGAR MAPLE TIME, VERMONT

MONTPELIER, CAPITAL OF VERMONT

Deep in the woods, Vermont's mountain streams beckon the angler to cast his fly with lures for brown and rainbow trout

ON THE MISSISQUOI, NORTHERN VERMONT

"Only an idle little stream,
Whose amber waters softly gleam,
Where I may wade through
woodland shade,
And cast the fly, and loaf,
and dream."

An angler's wish.

HENRY VAN DYKE

There is no joy like that of the deep woods. The woods have a power over the mind and a serenity of their own. No wonder we are always getting ready to go. No wonder we anxiously meet in the business offices of the men who are to make up the party, and discuss every detail of our anticipated pleasures...They are the woods of God—all right! They open to one vistas of sunlight falling slantwise through tall trees silent as the cathedral and almost as musical. The ripple of the falling water is musical. Weariness is not of the flesh alone. It is to the mind as well. These heal all the elements of a man, mind, soul and body. As I go along after having written some story of the woods—a trip up the Missisquoi for instance, I long to go back. It is the growing hope of the age, this love of the hills and forests.

ARTHUR G. STAPLES
A Tribute to the Woods

When the sugar-boilers get hungry, said a magazine of 1850, "as people are apt to do on occasions like this, a slice of brown bread, thickly covered with half-boiled sap, forms a very satisfying luncheon." Every step in sugaring is fun, but the big jollification comes at the end of the season. "The farmers take turns in inviting their neighbors to a sugaring-off, when the most interesting and fascinating of the population gather around the boiling sweetness and make merry while the hours slip away. It is estimated that the sugar-making season does more to encourage marriage than almost any other phenomenon in nature."

BARROWS MUSSEY
Vermont Heritage, 1975

Besides the lush greenery of its hills and dales, Vermonters are proudest of their native products: maple sugar, blue and white grained marble and granite—quarried in Barre, Proctor, Rutland and Graniteville

The quarries of New England have little gold in them, but the gnomes who dwell in the rock-ribbed hills of Vermont evidently possess the secret of wealth, for wherever the pickaxe strikes those quarries gold fills the coffers of those who develop the mines of marble and granite. Indeed the working of those quarries has become one of the most important industries of the eastern states, and is attracting a thrifty class of immigrants. This is especially true of the marble quarries of Vermont, which extend along the basin of Otter Creek. Marble of several varieties is found from Dorset to Burlington and beyond, and blue marble abounds east and west of the Green Mountains. But the veins of pure white fine-grained marble extend chiefly from Dorset to Middlebury. There is a watershed in Dorset where two streams arise within a few feet of each other. The Battenkill chooses a southerly course and enters the Hudson. The Otter Creek prefers a northerly direction, and meandering through a valley of surpassing loveliness, dominated by the imposing heights of Killington Peak, flows into Lake Champlain, and mingles its waters with the Gulf of St. Lawrence.

HARPER'S WEEKLY,
November 15, 1890

MARBLE QUARRIES AND MARBLE DRESSING, WEST RUTLAND AND PROCTOR

Rhode Island's Busy Towns & Seaports

PROVIDENCE ... ITS OLD LANDMARKS

... WESTMINSTER STREET ... MARKET

SQUARE ... ROCKY POINT ... PAWTUCKET

MILLS ... WOONSOCKET ... NEWPORT ...

ON THE BEACH

OLD HOMESTEAD.   AN OLD LANDMARK.   CITY MONUMENT.

IN PROVIDENCE

Rhode Island's Busy Towns & Seaports

NEATLY ALIGNED WITH THE SOUTHERN boundary of Massachusetts, flanking the eastern border of Connecticut, with waters of the Atlantic invading the state for 30 miles by way of Narragansett Bay—Rhode Island is the nation's smallest state and, from some viewpoints, the most extraordinary.

Providence, the capital, is also the largest city. Tiny as Rhode Island is, it possesses inestimable riches in Narragansett Bay, which is directly south of Providence and stretches for 30 miles to the Atlantic.

As early as 1524, the area is said to have been visited by Giovanni da Verrazano and, in 1614, by the Dutch Adrian Block. But it was not until 1636 that Roger Williams—having been banished for his freedom of thought by the Massachusetts Bay Colony in 1635—established the first settlement near Providence. He traveled on foot from Salem to Seekonk Plains and spent the winter with Indians there, becoming their advocate and friendly protector for as long as he lived. The next spring, Williams and five companions went by log-canoe on the Seekonk River, landing at what is today Slate Rock. Some Narragansett Indians, then the most powerful tribe in New England, were watching from a neighboring shore. Tradition has it that they greeted Williams with a friendly *"What Cheer!"*—words that later came to be the name of banks, public buildings, and various societies in the state.

A settlement was established near what is now Providence, which attracted a population notable for varied opinions, eager to think and speak as they wished.

In 1638, William Coddington, John Clarke, and Anne Hutchinson bought, with Williams's aid, the island of Aquidneck (now Rhode Island) from the Narragansetts, and established the settlement of Portsmouth. Factional differences developed and Coddington left the settlement. In 1638, he founded Newport, on the southwest side of the island.

The name of Providence reveals the spirit of its founders, and many street names indicate their ideals: Happy Street, Hope Street, Joy Street, Benefit Street.

By 1873, Providence had become New England's second city, one of the wealthiest— in proportion to its size—in the entire country.

From a sleepy town in the middle 1600s—a colony of idealists and freethinkers—to the most aristocratic and glamorous watering place less than two centuries later—Newport attracted the elite of Europe and America. Until the American Revolution, Newport was the commercial center, made vastly prosperous by the "Triangular Trade"—in rum, Negro slaves, and molasses.

Two hundred years ago, Newport had only one rival as the leading port in the Atlantic colonies: two hundred vessels were engaged in foreign trade; three hundred to four hundred more distributed the products unloaded on the docks to the coastal towns from Massachusetts to Virginia, providing merchants in Boston, New York and Philadelphia with their stocks. There was a line of packet ships running regularly between Newport and London.

Rhode Island's Bishop Berkeley wrote in 1728: "Newport is the most thriving in all America for bigness. I was never more agreeably surprised than at the sight of the town and the harbor." New Yorkers were admonished that, if they would only emulate the enterprise of Newporters, they might in time become formidable rivals.

What Newport became in the mid-1800s is too well known to require detailed description. Once more, Newport drew people from towns and cities, not for industry but for recreation. People of culture and wealth, foreign ministers, titled families, authors, actors, clergymen, politicians, highbred and fashionable women— Newport was the magnet that attracted them all. Great mansions—always called cottages— lined the avenues. Every morning the world's greatest steamships landed their elegant passengers; every afternoon a parade of luxurious equipages added to the splendor of the scene. Merchants built stately mansions on the water side, and their wainscoted walls, mahogany stairways, marble mantels, and tiled fireplaces still inspire awe.

At Rocky Point on Warwick Neck, passing from the Bay to Narragansett Pier, on what had been a waste with fishermen's old houses, thousands of bathers were to be seen. By the late eighties not fewer than eighteen hotels had been erected along the shore, some elegant and costly, of vast dimensions.

Samuel Slater, with the financial backing of Moses Brown, was a pioneer in establishing cotton textile mills built at Pawtucket in 1790.

From the turn-of-the-century grandeur of the mansions in Newport, to the crowded streets of factory towns, Rhode Island was a microcosm of all that was once most aristocratic, and also most typical of a thriving industrial state.

The nation's smallest state, with the longest name "The State of Rhode Island and Providence Plantations," is unique in many ways . . .

In the winter of 1636 Williams made his way to Narragansett Bay and there, having bought the land from the Indians, he and his followers built the town of Providence. There they founded their society on the principles for which Williams had fought. Each head of a family was to have an equal voice with all the others in the government. In religion, every individual was to be completely free to worship as he thought best; and there was a complete separation of church and state. The activities of the state were strictly limited to civil affairs.

In 1647, when the town of Providence united with the towns of Warwick, Portsmouth, and Newport to form the colony of Rhode Island, these principles were written into the constitution of the colony, establishing "a government held by the free and voluntarie consent of all, or the greater part of the free inhabitants," and providing for freedom of conscience and separation of church and state. Thus Rhode Island, under the inspiration and guidance of Roger Williams, became the great pilot experiment in American democracy and religious toleration.

C. BRIDENBAUGH
William Penn, Founder of Colonies

WESTMINSTER STREET.

MARKET SQUARE AND "WHAT CHEER" BUILDING, PROVIDENCE

*. . . having had two capitals, both Newport
and Providence, as late as 1900 when the new
state capitol was built in the latter city*

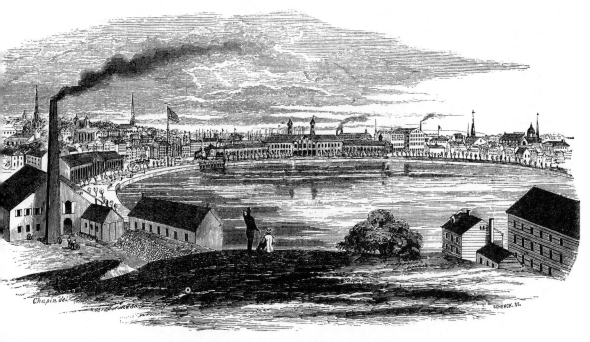

PROVIDENCE, FROM SMITH'S HILL

PROVIDENCE, FROM SOUTHERN SUBURBS

BREAKWATER, NARRAGANSETT PIER

"Little Rhody" is a unique world. Physically, it ranks as America's smallest state. Until New Jersey surpassed it recently, it was the most densely populated of all the states, and can safely be called the "most ethnic." Finally, it is the most consistently Democratic state in its voting habits. The compactness is illustrated by Rhode Island's measurements: only 48 miles from north to south, and an even more modest 37 miles from east to west. These 1,214 square miles could be contained in New York State 41 times, in Texas 227 times, in Alaska almost 500 times. . . . A word should be said about Providence's watery site and its port. The city is located on the Providence and Seekunk Rivers, which flow into and form the head of Narragansett Bay. This was traditionally Providence's window to the world, and the history books are replete with romantic references to the era when tall-masted Indiamen and other ships crowded the harbor. One important improvement of recent years was the construction of a hurricane barrier, a sensible insurance against disasters which have plagued the city in the past.

NEAL R. PEIRCE
*The New England States,
1976*

Pawtucket owes its fame as the birthplace of America's cotton industry, in 1790—to a young British mill apprentice, Samuel Slater . . .

Simultaneously with the sudden rise of the Cotton Kingdom in the South, Samuel Slater, a cotton-mill operative from England, was in Rhode Island trying to remember how the textile machinery which he had tended in the old country had been built, for England prohibited the export of any of the machines lest the industry might be set up elsewhere. Slater was successful, machines were built here, and the foundations laid for the growth of the New England textile mills. Great as the differences between the sections had already been, they were to be increasingly emphasized during the next half century.

JAMES TRUSLOW ADAMS
The Epic of America, 1931

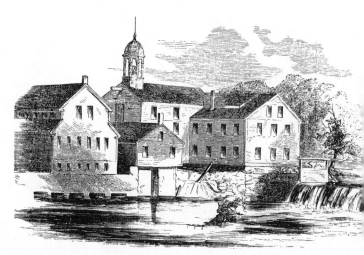

OLD SLATER MILL, PAWTUCKET

With some justification, Rhode Island claims to be the birthplace of the American factory system. And it was at Pawtucket in 1790 that Samuel Slater—financed by Moses Brown of the famous Rhode Island merchant family—reproduced the Arkwright machines of England, starting the young country's first mechanized cotton mill. Within 25 years of Slater's coming, according to one account, Rhode Island Mills were turning out more than 27 million yards of cloth a year and providing jobs for 26,000 operatives (including many child laborers). Together with cotton milling, the woolen and worsted industry flourished in 19th-and early 20th-century Rhode Island. Until the 1940s, when the exodus of mills to the South hit its peak, spinning and weaving was the dominant industry of Rhode Island. It was also the state's Achilles heel, because the ethnic stock workers were paid appallingly low wages; the image of the old textile industry, as one labor leader described it to me, was of dim 25-watt lighting and creaking old elevators in rambling, often decrepit mill buildings. In the 1920s, 90,000 men and women—three-fifths of the Rhode Island factory employment—were in textiles; in the last few years, the total has been scarcely 18,000.

NEAL R. PEIRCE
The New England States,
1976

THE FALLS AND MILLS ON THE PAWTUCKET RIVER

DUNNELL MILLS, PAWTUCKET

*. . . whose successful operation in cotton spinning
was duplicated in neighboring Woonsocket, a town
off in the extreme northeast corner of the state*

MAIN STREET, PAWTUCKET

"New England," wrote Bernard DeVoto nearly twenty years ago, "is a finished place...it is the first American section to be finished, to achieve stability in the conditions of its life. It is the first old civilization and the first permanent civilization in America." Obviously this comment suffers somewhat from exaggeration, but it does point up the fact that there are areas in the nations that have become comparatively old economically—and as such, despite their prestige, raise special problems. These areas are not limited to the six northeastern states, nor even to the Middle Atlantic area...

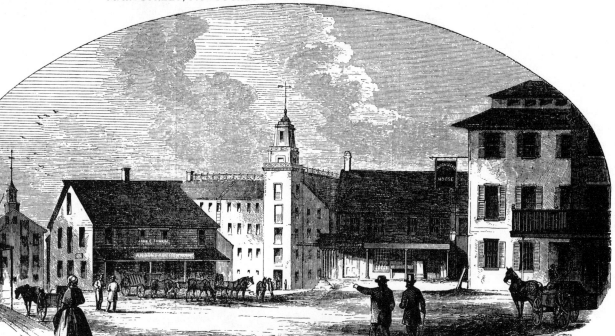

POST OFFICE SQUARE, WOONSOCKET

WOONSOCKET COMPANY'S MILL

...But the impact of economic maturity and economic stability in industrial development without a corresponding stability in employment is to be found primarily in an area such as New England, where industrialization has been more pronounced and more continuous. The results are that machinery is old, methods are perforce old, and too frequently management is old. Community after community has relied for years upon one or two industries, and a decline in the world market for the products of these industries may take place. Some fast-growing industries have settled elsewhere, leaving areas of serious unemployment and of economic stagnation in our generally prosperous country.

JOHN F. KENNEDY

New England Industry, 1953

Before the Revolution, Newport prospered as its skippers plied the i. famous triangular trade: slaves from Africa; molasses and rum via t. Caribbean. In the Gilded Age socialites built their "cottages" he

The great event in the fashionable world was a Newport ball. A lady who had married a man of cultivation and taste, a member of one of New York's oldest families, who had inherited from her father an enormous fortune, was at once seized with the ambition to take and hold a brilliant social position, to gratify which she built one of the handsomest houses in this city, importing interiors from Europe for it and such old Spanish tapestries as had never before been introduced into New York; after which she went to Newport and bought a beautiful villa on Bellevue Avenue and there gave, in the grounds of that villa, the handsomest ball that had ever been given there....All Newport was present to give brilliancy to the scene. Everything was to be European; so one supped at small tables as at a ball in Paris all through the night.

WARD MC ALLISTER

Society As I Have Found It,
1890

ON THE BEACH

NEWPORT, FROM THE BAY

The Connecticut Valley & Villages

WINDSOR LOCKS . . . SAYBROOK . . .

THE CONNECTICUT . . . MIDDLETOWN . . .

HARTFORD . . . STATE HOUSE . . .

TRINITY COLLEGE . . . PUTNEY . . .

SUGAR LOAF MOUNTAIN . . .

BELLOWS FALLS . . . GREENFIELD . . .

SUNDERLAND . . . NEW HAVEN . . .

YALE COLLEGE . . . SALISBURY . . .

ALONG THE SOUND . . . NEW LONDON . . .

NORWALK . . . BRIDGEPORT . . .

STRATFORD . . . MILFORD

WINDSOR LOCKS, CONNECTICUT RIVER

The Connecticut Valley & Villages

OFTEN CALLED "QUEEN OF NEW England rivers"—the Connecticut flows from a trio of small lakes in northeast New Hampshire for nearly 400 miles, to empty in Long Island Sound. Along its course, it gathers waters of many small, sparkling streams, and provides water power for countless industries. Creating a rich, alluvial valley and prosperous farmlands, and inspiring the settlement of many villages and towns, the Connecticut River defines the boundaries of New Hampshire and Vermont, flows all across Massachusetts, and bisects Connecticut, enriching the land every mile of the way.

Three men—Thomas Hooker, Samuel Stone, and John Haynes—the first two "reverends," the third a wealthy landowner who was elected governor of Massachusetts Bay, felt cramped in the Massachusetts Bay Colony and declared that "the bent of their spirits" prompted them to leave. They marched across country, guided only by a compass, and reached the Connecticut river, settling three towns: Hartford, Windsor, and Wethersfield.

Previously, the Dutch navigator, Adriaen Block, had sailed into Long Island Sound, and discovered the mouth of the Connecticut river in 1614. The Dutch built a fort in 1633 but, constantly harried by the English, abandoned the settlement in 1654.

The fertile valley inspired glowing reports,

and a second group of Puritans set forth from Cambridge, numbering about a hundred men, women, and children. One chronicle recounts their hardships: "On foot, through a hideous, trackless wilderness, over mountains, through swamps, thickets, and rivers, with no cover but the heavens, nor any lodgings but what simple nature affords, subsisting en route on milk from the cattle they drove with them. They carried packs, arms, and some utensils, and were nearly a fortnight on the journey." This group also settled in Hartford. The report summarizes: "This adventure was the more remarkable, as many of this company were persons of figure, who had lived in affluence and honor in England, and were strangers to danger and fatigue."

A third group of Puritans—these from London—came seeking a site for a trading town to compete with New York and Boston. Their leaders, Theophilus Eaton and the Reverend John Davenport, selected New Haven. This colony spread along the river and crossed Long Island Sound. A written constitution, called the Fundamental Orders of Connecticut and New Haven, was evolved in 1639 and served until 1662, when Charles II issued a corporate charter which remained the law for colony and state until 1818. Representatives from three Connecticut river towns—Hartford, Windsor, and Wethersfield—had adopted the fundamental orders for "an orderly and decent government according to God." Any householder of "honest conversation" was admitted to town meetings. The desire for more and better land, rather than religious differences, prompted many of the migrations to Connecticut. A number of settlements burgeoned along the river and the sound. The government functioned smoothly, except for a brief period during the administration of Sir Edmund Andros. On his royal appointment as Governor General of New England, he sent word that Connecticut must surrender its charter. This request being ignored, Sir Edmund journeyed to Hartford with sixty British troops. The assembly was in session. The governor general was greeted courteously. The charter was laid on a table. Suddenly, the lights were extinguished, a Captain Wadsworth of the assembly snatched the charter and disappeared into the night. This led to the tale, still told, of Hartford's famous "charter oak." Like the great elm of Boston Common, Hartford's oak is said to have been of fabulous age, a thousand years, with a diameter of seven feet. In a hollow root of the old tree, Captain Wadsworth is reputed to have secreted the precious charter.

The Connecticut River separates the state in almost equal—east and west—sections, generally referred to as the east and west "highlands." Artists and craftsmen were drawn to Connecticut early in colonial days, and small manufacturing projects sprang up, attracted by the plentiful water power. Villages were settled all along the river shores and throughout the fertile valley. But, although it is known for its rural beauty, Connecticut's wealth is derived overwhelmingly from its industry. Alexis de Toqueville's summary is widely known: "Connecticut...the little spot ...that makes the clock peddler, the schoolmaster, and the senator. The first, gives you time; the second, tells you what to do with it; the third, makes your law and your civilization."

Famous for making firearms and ammunition since the American Revolution, Connecticut—often called the "gadget" state—produces many manufactures requiring special skills: revolvers, clocks and watches, silverware, auger bits, ball bearings, typewriters, electrical products, as well as hats, saddlery, coffins, and submarines.

Chicopee is another charming river town on the route to Holyoke—early famous for the Mount Holyoke "female seminary." Here are enchanting glimpses of Northampton on the right and, more distant, Amherst with its prestigious college, founded in 1821. One of the most beautiful cities on the river is Brattleboro, in Vermont, where the water earned such a reputation for purity that it inspired the establishment of several "water-cure" sanitariums. In the heart of the mountains—where the White River empties into the Connecticut, at White River Junction—the distance is short to Hanover, noted for Dartmouth College, chartered by royal grant in 1769. Dartmouth has many distinguished graduates, among them Daniel Webster.

From Saybrook on Long Island Sound, to Stewartstown on the Canadian border, hundreds of settlements owe their beginnings and steady growth to the Connecticut River and the many little rivers that flow into it. With the Connecticut, the Housatonic and the Naugatuck merit mention. Each in its meanderings collects a multitude of smaller rivers and streams. Together, richly, they fertilize and power the state.

Flowing purposefully from near the Canadian border due south to the Long Island Sound, the Connecticut River divides New Hampshire and Vermont . . .

This isn't a piece about Middletown or Anyburg or Sauk Center. The country towns here in New England all bear a family resemblance to one another, but they also have individual characters that can be learned only by living in them. They are more or less united as communities, more or less friendly to newcomers, more or less dominated by cliques that are more or less conservative and sometimes corrupt. But all of them are different from small towns in other parts of the country, and I suspect that all of them have been rapidly changing since the war, in fashions that are not always apparent to their own inhabitants. . .Sheridan is a town only in the New England sense; in New York it would be an unincorporated village, in Pennsylvania a township and farther west nothing more than a school district. It consists of about twenty-five square miles of land shaped like a narrow slice of pie—a valley ten miles along with a lake in the south, farmland in the north and a range of wooded hills on either side. The back roads are full of abandoned farms like those described in Slater Brown's novel, "The Burning Wheel." North of the village, locally called the Center, there are twenty fairly prosperous dairy farms. Summer cottages are clustered along the shores of the lake and scattered through the hills. The winter population is about 450.

MALCOLM COWLEY   *Town Report: 1942*

SAYBROOK

THE CONNECTICUT, ABOVE MIDDLETOWN

. . . the entire length of each state, continuing through Massachusetts and Connecticut. Its valley of enchanting beauty . . . famous for many history-rich towns

MAIN STREET BRIDGE, HARTFORD

The Indian word *Quinnehtukqut* meant: "Beside the long tidal river." The state of Connecticut, as now constituted, is well served by rivers—7600 miles of them; but the one from which it takes its name, along which it was originally settled, and which is still its central axis, is the Connecticut. "The Great River," the early settlers called it. Perhaps this was partly because the Indian word was too much of a mouthful, but it was also an honest evaluation. It is indeed a Great River, the longest in New England. Up at the Canadian border, where it rises, it is just a trickle, but it picks up force and volume all the way down its 360-mile course between New Hampshire and Vermont, through Massachusetts, and then through Connecticut to Long Island Sound. Dropping some 1600 feet en route, it provides the water power on which are based many of New England's cities—Bellows Falls, Brattleboro, Turners Falls, Greenfield, Holyoke, Springfield, Windsor Locks, Hartford, Middletown. These are important cities in the economic life of New England, and the Great River made them so.

The broad central valley through which the river flows for two thirds of its course through Connecticut is the heart of the state, a rich, busy, self-sufficient middle ground between an extended New York suburbia to the west and a hilly hinterland to the east. Some of the state's greatest industrial cities are here—though one hardly thinks of them as river towns; and the center of population of the state is only slightly to the southwest of the valley. Here, too, are the state's richest agricultural lands.

ARTHUR BARTLETT
American Panorama, 1947

HARTFORD, FROM EAST SIDE OF THE RIVER

*At Connecticut's capital, Hartford, sternwheelers
once transported luxuriant produce of the region—
especially leaf tobacco—downriver to New York markets*

The river traffic consisted mostly of flatboats, occasionally with sails and poling devices to get them back upstream, but more commonly the flatboats were broken up for their timber when they arrived at Hartford. A few small steamboats managed to cope with the rapids above Springfield, the earliest one on the Connecticut River invented and built by Samuel Morey in 1793, six years after John Fitch's original invention, of which Morey was unaware, and fourteen years before Robert Fulton's. Stern-wheelers built by Thomas Blanchard thrived briefly on the Connecticut after 1826. Charles Dickens wrote a deprecatory account of riding a small steamboat downriver among February ice-cakes from Springfield to Hartford during his American tour. But the most active steamboating on the Connecticut River was not in Massachusetts, but rather below Hartford, where service to New York by the Connecticut Steamboat Company persisted long after the railroads arrived. In Massachusetts most Connecticut River traffic was of the canalboat type. Tobacco, potatoes, celery and onions were the agricultural products, especially leaf tobacco for cigar wrappers, on which Connecticut valley farmers grew wealthy from 1830 on.

STEAMERS ON THE CONNECTICUT, HARTFORD

HENRY F. HOWE
*Massachusetts:
There She Is—Behold Her, 1960*

HARTFORD, FROM COLT'S FACTORY

While various industries developed, as early as the eighteenth century, Hartford prospered as the center for underwriting, especially of casualty insurance

STATE HOUSE, MAIN STREET, HARTFORD

TRINITY COLLEGE, HARTFORD

The lamps which lined the streets of Hartford sent forth an icy breath-like light. Here, there could be no sympathy, no tenderness, no mood to warm a passing stranger. The night was young—but it had settled as if to stay forever. Such a night was March 5, 1860. It was when Abraham Lincoln came to Hartford, gaunt and tall, and supperless, but fired by a greater appetite—into the state where once lived John Brown, who now "lay mouldering;" and Harriet Beecher Stowe, whose battlecry for freedom was fanning flames across the eastern horizon. This great and really rended heart must surely have opened wider beneath the soot-stained, loosely-draping coat as he rode down Main Street in his carriage and perceived the strength of his support. Yankee men and women had forsaken warming hearths this cold and winter-ending evening to blend their sense of right with his. For he had spoken—this gentle, worn and weary man—and Yankee hearts went out to him. The torchlights swept around him like a sudden gust of flaming wind, and Lincoln spoke again. "The boys are wide awake," he said; "let's call them Wide-Awakes." The name spread through the nation. That's how the Wide-Awakes first formed—to gird themselves to battle for what they considered right. "Right, Eternal Right, makes might, and as we understand our duty, so do it."

Highways & Byways of
Connecticut, 1947

*Along the river's winding course, every town
had its grist mill, where the plunging waters
were dammed to provide needed water power*

OLD MILL, PUTNEY

The mills were everywhere. The town where I have spent the pleasantest of my summers is far to the north; it has 500 inhabitants and a single woodworking mill. A century ago it had 1200 inhabitants and the two creeks powered a gristmill, a sawmill, a planing and turning mill, a fulling mill, a fanning mill, and one of those primordial "machine shops" that would do anything the surrounding market wanted done. What ended this happiest period of the industrial revolution was not only the spread of steam and, later on, of electric power that made industrial concentrations economical, but even more the development of the railroad network. Massachusetts and Connecticut, with their greater railroad mileage, developed the mill town as we now know it—and learned the vulnerability of a one-industry economy when later shifts came.

BERNARD DE VOTO

New England, from
The Romance of North America, 1958

BELLOWS FALLS

With the passing years, old mill sites display only a pile of stones, half-rotted wheels and timber, relics of a civilization that has passed

For the Yankees who turned to the glacial waterfalls had found the genius of their breed. We may now return to those masonry dams that are the vestiges of another age. They are on all rivers and creeks and on some brooks so small that you can hardly believe the evidence. Beside them are brick walls it would take high explosives or a vagabond hurricane with its torrents of rain to demolish, though roofs and windows have been gone for two generations or more. The walls are those of little mills that were powered by the dams, the mills to which the Yankee genius brought precision, versatility, and unsurpassed craftsmanship. The Yankees were predestined smiths, mechanics, artificers, contrivers, innovators. The direct and orderly progression of machine processes was their intellectual idiom. Indeed it was their spiritual well-being, for what is the logic of machines if it is not the identical economy, exactness, propriety and neatness that I have already called elegance? At the village green, the exquisite steeple and the scrubbed stoop with a pumpkin on it; in the shipyards, the lines of the clippers; in the shop, a turret lathe or a drop forge growing ever more complex and automatic as Yankee logic works out its functions.

BERNARD DE VOTO
New England, from
The Romance of North America, 1958

STEVENS BROOK, BARNET

WHETSTONE BROOK, BRATTLEBORO

Upstream, where the river narrows, its mood changes from a placid stream, feeding fertile meadows, to plunge precipitously between granite boulders . . .

Tinkling rills of the hills,
Rippling down the trails,
From the crags of mountain-tops
Into wooded dales,

Joining brooks in lily nooks
Flashing foamy white,
Purling round the stony pools
In a wild delight!

On-swirling, upward-curling,
Plumed with tossing spray,
Dancing, teasing, frolicking,
And wandering away.

Into streams deep in dreams,
Curved in slender grace,
Shadow-flecked and glimmering
In veils of leafy lace!

Thus the waters, sparkling, darkling,
Like our myriad lives—
Brooks a-play, streams a-dream,
While the river strives.

Toward the free, unbounded sea
They rush victoriously;
Like human souls, merged into great
Unfathomed unity.

MILDRED HOBBS
Little Rivers

THE WEST BRANCH OF BELLOWS FALLS

CONNECTICUT VALLEY, FROM ROCKY MOUNTAIN, GREENFIELD

*. . . where wooden structures spanned the river,
including quaint covered bridges, many of which
are still in service a century and a half later*

SUGAR LOAF MOUNTAIN, FROM SUNDERLAND

This elegance is the swept and garnished New England countryside, the houses and town halls and meetinghouses whose white paint is spiritual dignity, the fanlights of the mansions, the scrubbed stoops (with a pumpkin on them at harvesttime) of the farmhouses themselves, sited not only so that they are sheltered from the prevailing wind but so that they take in the vista of the creek curving toward the fold in the hills. It is almost inconceivable now that the hill farms were once a wheat country and a sheep country. That period could not possibly last; the upland soil washed into the creeks long ago...The farmers who did not go west moved to the valleys and to whatever flatland New England has, mainly in Connecticut, Down East in Maine, and along the Connecticut River. Sometimes they moved their town halls and meetinghouses with them. Valley soil, truck gardening, and dairy farming saved the stricken agriculture. Commercial farming, with the increased efficiency of specialized one-crop agriculture but also with its greater risks, took the place of subsistence farming...In summer the Connecticut Valley is wonderfully pleasing striations of green and white, the onion fields and the cheesecloth tents that shade the tobacco fields. But the truth is that not many of the original Yankees were talented farmers; their genius was of a different kind.

BERNARD DE VOTO

*The Romance of
North America, 1958*

WHITE RIVER JUNCTION

*Long Island Sound has a hundred towns and villages—
each an entity, important industrially, or
as a seaport or summer resort . . .*

The flames which once had glowed on Norwalk slopes, like falls of crimson water, as all the city was destroyed by foreign soldiers, had long since paled. A new and prosperous city had sprung up from rubbled ashes, a city filled with industry and pride...And yet, what's this we see? A large, impressive concourse of grim, determined people is gathered on the village green. No human tears fall here. Their heavy clothes are gathered warmly against the winter's cold. Small children snuggle safely in their rugged parents' arms. And quiet lies on every side, as silently as midnight on a desert. But time for everything relentlessly arrives— and time has come. The last farewells are spoken— the last endearing glances interchanged....The same mute gleam of inquiry and question fills the eye and trembles on the lips of everyone there. But no one words it—no one whispers —the thought in every mind. Instead, we hear the somber strains of a Doxology, as voices rise in ever-growing chant. And, slowly, the long cavalcade of prairie wagons joins the file of wagons rolling by. And many Norwalk families wind Westward towards Ohio's Firelands— their new home to be. A grateful nation's gift of homage for their gallant sacrifice in war, when all homesteads burned. New lands for old—new worlds to conquer. And thus Norwalk in Ohio was founded —by pioneers from ravaged Norwalk in Connecticut.

*Highways & Byways of
Connecticut, 1947*

THE VILLAGE GREEN, NORWALK

MAIN STREET, NORWALK

. . . where the joys of sailing, swimming, oystering and fishing combine the aspects of both land and sea, providing abundant year-round pleasures

My life is like a stroll
  upon the beach,
As near the ocean's edge
  as I can go;
My tardy steps its waves
  sometimes o'erreach,
Sometimes I stay to let
  them overflow.
My sole employment 'tis,
  and scrupulous care,
To place my gains beyond
  the reach of tides;
Each smoother pebble, and
  each shell more rare,
Which ocean kindly to my
  hand confides,
I have but few companions
  on the shore,
They scorn the strand who
  sail upon the sea;
Yet oft I think the ocean
  they've sailed o'er
Is deeper known upon
  the strand to me.
The middle sea contains no
  crimson dulse,
Its deeper waves cast up
  no pearls to view;
Along the shore my hand
  is on its pulse,
And I converse with many
  a shipwrecked crew.

HENRY DAVID THOREAU

NORWALK, ROTON POINT AND WILSONS POINT, ON THE SOUND

The coastal towns of Bridgeport, Stratford, and Milford are steeped in antiquarian lore—their current charm intermixed with ancient adventures, bloody battles, defeats and victories

We are going to weave our tale from all the worn but still glossy threads from the life of P.T. Barnum. It is only fitting that we visit Bridgeport, to think of this great showman and explore the many unexpected facets which historic light casts on his name. For Barnum, founder of "The Greatest Show on Earth," is rightly Bridgeport's most loved son. With him as leader, Bridgeport grew to present size with all her vast and teeming, thriving industry which makes her name renowned throughout the world.

Settled in 1639, the town of Stratford, first known as Cupheag, with its shading elms and old white houses, became a constant center of startling events. For this was the home of the Johnsons—the Reverend Doctor Samuel Johnson, and his erudite son, William Samuel. Dr. Johnson became a president of King's College in New York, and one of Columbia University's founders. His son became Connecticut's first senator and a celebrated lawyer.

Milford was also settled in 1639 and became a favorite recreation spot for people who value gastronomical delights. Milford—land of oysters—Indians from many miles around came each year for "salting" as they called it. This consisted solely of downing as many oysters as the sated appetite could hold. And, though times have changed, Milford is still proud of her succulent, juicy seafood.

Highways & Byways of Connecticut, 1947

SCENES IN BRIDGEPORT, STRATFORD, AND MILFORD

*In New London, a privateers' rendezvous during the Revolution
—partially burned in 1781, blockaded by the British in 1812
—shipping, shipbuilding and whaling brought maritime prosperity*

NEW LONDON, FROM THE SHORE ROAD

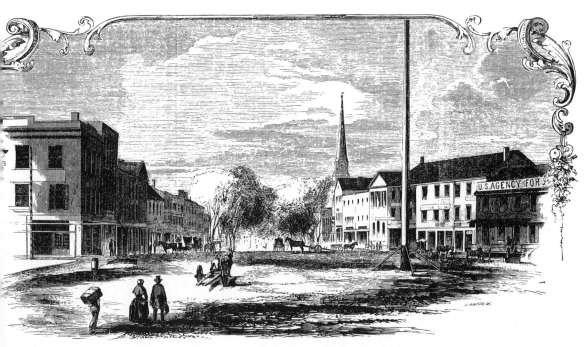

STATE STREET, NEW LONDON

What tempestuous threads of history she has woven in the over-all pattern of romance! To wander on her crowded, crooked water-front byways or view the silent walks on now stilled captains' homes is to bring to mind a hundred different memories of excitement and adventure. The air is redolent with salt and spices—mingled with molasses and the sharper tang of tar and hempen ropes. New London is the cradle of all men who brave the deep. Rendezvous of privateers, port of pirates—graceful sloops and white-rigged schooners once bobbed where submarines and ships of war now lie at anchor. For centuries her never-quiet streets have echoed to the roystering gayness of heart-free, sea-bound men. In 1847, whaling ships rocked restlessly, tugging at their hawsers—for New London, then, was at the peak of her great and prosperous whaling trade. Seventy some odd ships and barks, brigs and schooners, sailed the seven seas in search of gold and danger. The gushing flow of whale and sperm oil, the floundering seals and sea-elephants which slithered from the decks of ice-caked ships, were only mute reminders of the perils they had faced. From the Southern seas to Greenland and the regions east of Cape Horn. To the Arctic where the freezing floes closed in like whitened, death-trap jaws. For, as the old Gazette enthusiastically exhorted: "Now, my horse jockeys, beat your cattle and horses into spears, lances, harpoons and whaling gear, and let us all strike out; many spouts ahead."

*Highways & Byways of
Connecticut, 1947*

In Connecticut's northwest corner, at Salisbury, busy blast furnaces gave valuable aid to the struggling colonies in the Revolutionary War

Salisbury! Salisbury once was the Birmingham of this vast country. Salisbury, where Mt. Riga stands in all her humble majesty and lonely splendor. If we had traveled here in 1847 we would have seen an awesome sight. The last long, flickering flame of ruddy light on Old Forge Pond, which must have glowed among the mountain fastnesses like a bowl of ruby wine, as stillness fell once more across the rugged peaks. The only burning forge gone out when progress moved the thriving trade to Salisbury streets beneath. In 1847 railroads came to shift the source of industry to more accessible spots. But progress could not change the fame which earlier days had brought—when Salisbury men climbed heavily up these hills to seek the ore and bring it into light. The elevated hills. The deep, extensive limestone valleys. If we had been there then, we would have seen the last full saddle bags of ore going down those rocky lanes on teams of oxen—the same dirt road which bore the weight of cannon ball and cannon—of anchor chains and anchors. For here it was they forged the anchor of the "Constitution," and six strong, straining yoke of oxen bore it down beneath the shadow of the western ridges of the Hudson. But now you see, instead of belching flame and cinder, the white little houses standing forth against the stain of forest green on hill-tops. The forges in the hills lie dormant as time moves on—but Salisbury is a proud and prosperous town.

Highways & Byways of Connecticut, 1947

SITE OF REVOLUTIONARY FOUNDRY, SALISBURY

TWIN LAKES, SALISBURY

New Haven—which boasts a beautiful green and Yale's elm-shaded campus—is notable for Yankee inventiveness. Here Eli Whitney helped spark the industrial revolution

YALE COLLEGE, NEW HAVEN

RAILROAD STATION, NEW HAVEN

New Haven—beehive of industry, amidst whose teeming streets, incongruously, sleep vestiges of venerable grandeur and hoary nostalgic stories of the past—remnants of a most prodigious history. New Haven—settled in 1638—what a fabulous wealth of romance and great deeds lies here where Yale presents the benefits of faultless culture to students garnered from the whole wide world. Her solid red hills stand sentinels, in lofty meditation, above the still-unfolding mysteries of her elm-lined streets. The West and Mill and Quinnipiac Rivers flow mutely by. New Haven fairly reeks of histrionic lore. There are episodic portraits of redskins in the forest—of colonial courage and ingenious acts of skill. Bravery and treason walk hand in hand through the hushed shadows of the alleys. Shades of Roger Sherman and Benedict Arnold, of Baldwins, Davenports, and Hookers haunt the narrow byways where inventiveness has lodged since early days. Here came into being the first type foundry, and the first successful milling machines. The first engine lathes, and the first polished copper—the first commercial switchboard and the first machine for dipping wooden matches. This is the town for erudition, for Winchester rifles and Sargent locks—for New Haven clocks and numerous other manufactures. From 1701 to 1875 New Haven was the joint capital of the state and through the panorama of her iridescent past float images of all America's elite.

Highways & Byways of
Connecticut, 1947

Inspired by the Romanesque tradition of southern France, H. H. Richardson—one of the true geniuses of American architecture—gave Yale a new face, many years before it acquired Wrexham and Harkness Memorial

First the visitor will observe the remarkable beauty of the campus or that portion of the University bounded by Chapel, High, Elm and Cottage streets. Generations ago rows of elms were planted there, beneath whose wide-spreading branches thousands of students have wended their way, and in whose shade many of America's most learned scholars, distinguished statesmen and eminent teachers have received the education which aided them to become the great public benefactors that they were.

W.E. DECROW
Yale and the City of Elms

RECITATION HALL AND NEW LIBRARY, YALE COLLEGE, NEW HAVEN

List of Authors

Adams, James Truslow, 82
Aldrich, Thomas Bailey, 53

Bartlett, Arthur, 89
Beston, Henry, 5
Bridenbaugh, C., 80
Burroughs, Nathaniel, 61

Cobb, Irwin S., 14
Cochran, T.C., 47
Cowley, Malcolm, 88

Davidson, Marshall B., 43
De Voto, Bernard, 92, 93, 95
Dickens, Charles, 30
Downing, A.J., 45
Earle, Alice Morse, 42

Frost, Robert, 62

Goldberg, Issac, 27

Hobbs, Mildred, 94
Holmes, Oliver Wendell, 19
Hornung, Clarence P., 34-35
Howe, Henry F., 48, 50, 55, 90

Jewett, Sarah Orne, 14
Johnson, Rossiter, 70, 71, 72

Kennedy, John F., 83

Lee, Eliza Buckminster, 49
Longfellow, Henry Wadsworth, 53

McAllister, Ward, 84
McCord, David, 20, 21, 22, 26, 36
Morison, Samuel Eliot, 25, 31, 102
Mussey, Barrows, 75

Nutting, Wallace, 54

Peirce, Neal R., 18, 81, 82

Rich, Louise Dickinson, 4, 10, 11, 12
Rideing, W.H., 73
Roberts, Kenneth, 7
Robinson, Henry Morton, 28

Schauffler, Robert Haven, 56
Staples, Arthur G., 75
Steinbeck, John, 6

Thaxter, Celia, 9
Thoreau, Henry David, 13, 46, 97

Van Dyke, Henry, 75

Whittier, John Greenleaf, 32

Acknowledgments

James Truslow Adams. *The Epic of America*. Copyright 1931, 1933. Copyright renewed 1959 by James Truslow Adams. Reprinted by permission of Little, Brown & Co.

Henry Beston. *The Outermost House*, by Henry Beston. Copyright 1928, 1949, 1956 by Henry Beston. Copyright 1977 by Elizabeth C. Beston. Reprinted by permission of Holt, Rinehart, and Winston Publishers.

John Burroughs. *The Heart of Burrough's Journals*. Copyright 1928. Reprinted by permission of Houghton, Mifflin Company.

Nathaniel Burt. *The Perennial Philadelphians: The Anatomy of American Aristocracy*. Copyright 1963 by Nathaniel Burt. Reprinted by permission of Little, Brown & Co.

Marshall B. Davidson. *Life in America*. Copyright 1951 by Marshall B. Davidson. Reprinted by permission of Houghton, Mifflin Company.

G. Fox & Company. *Highways and Byways of Connecticut*. Copyright 1947 by G. Fox & Company. Reprinted by permission of G. Fox & Company.

Clarence P. Hornung. *Wheels Across America*. Copyright 1959 by A.S. Barnes and Co.

Henry F. Howe. *Massachusetts, There She Is — Behold Her*. Copyright 1960 by Henry F. Howe. Reprinted by permission of Harper & Row Publishers, Inc.

Barrows Mussey. *Vermont Heritage*. Copyright 1975. Reprinted by permission of the author.

David McCord. *About Boston*. Copyright 1948, 1973 by David McCord. Reprinted by permission of Little, Brown & Co.

The Pageant of America series. Copyright by U.S. Publishers Assn. Reprinted by permission of the publishers.

Neal R. Peirce. *The New England States*. Copyright 1976, 1972 by Neal R. Peirce. Selections are reprinted with the permission of W.W. Norton & Company, Inc.

Louise Dickinson Rich. *The Coast of Maine*. Copyright 1956, 1962 by Louise Dickinson Rich. Reprinted by permission of Curtis Brown Ltd.

Kenneth Roberts. *Trending Into Maine*. Copyright 1938. Reprint, Down East Books, 1977.

John Steinbeck. *Travels with Charley in Search of America*. Copyright 1961, 1962 by Curtis Publishing Co., Inc. Copyright 1962 by John Steinbeck. Reprinted by permission of The Viking Press.

Notes